Praise for *Safe Haven in America*

———

"I thank Michael Wildes for his counsel in reviewing my own path to the American Dream, for his knowledge and professional dedication, not to mention his warmth and concern. He has shown himself to be a scholar in his field."

—*First Lady Melania Trump*

———

"Only once does the Hebrew Bible command us to love our neighbour. Yet on thirty-six times, it commands us to love the stranger. A neighbour is one we love because he or she is like us. A stranger is one we are taught to love precisely because he or she is not like us. Throughout this fascinating book, Michael shows his love for the 'stranger' and his passion for opening the doors of America to the world."

—*Rabbi Lord Jonathan Sacks, Chief Rabbi, United Kingdom*

———

"I appreciate Leon Wildes and his son Michael from when they handled my friend John Lennon's green card, right up to Michael's handling of my very own visa. Their legend as champions of international immigration is well-deserved."

—*Pele, soccer legend/icon*

———

"As the cases in this book show, Michael Wildes continues the struggle—in courtrooms, in the halls of government, and in front of the cameras, fighting for the values to which I hope our country will always remain true."

—*Alan Dershowitz, Harvard Law professor and author of* Taking the Stand: My Life in the Law

———

"I needed an expert lawyer to resolve my immigration issues, and I found him in Michael Wildes. Michael's book is a must-read for history buffs and anyone who cares at all about immigration, human rights, and dignity. Michael Wildes is a great lawyer. Loved his history and his advice! If his family was good enough for John Lennon, they're good enough for me!"

—*Boy George, musician/performer*

———

"With respect to the specialized and highly complex area of immigration litigation, there is no better lawyer than Michael Wildes. Period."

—*Benjamin Brafman, criminal defense lawyer*

———

"Any competent lawyer may be fine for common immigration problems. But when it's a question of life or death—like defecting from an absolutist state—I'd want no one but Michael Wildes on my side."

—*Mohammed Khilewi, Saudi diplomat/defector*

———

SAFE HAVEN
IN AMERICA

*Battles to Open the
Golden Door*

Michael Wildes

Cover design by Elmarie Jara/ABA Design.
Interior design by Amanda Fry/ABA Design.

Printed in the United States of America.

22 21 20 19 18   5 4 3 2 1

ISBN: 978-1-64105-189-7

Discounts are available for books ordered in bulk. Special consideration is given to state bars, CLE programs, and other bar-related organizations. Inquire at Book Publishing, ABA Publishing, American Bar Association, 321 N. Clark Street, Chicago, Illinois 60654-7598.

www.shopABA.org

Dedicated to my parents, Ruth and Leon Wildes,
both children of immigrants, with gratitude
for their exceptional encouragement,
guidance, and love.

Contents

Acknowledgments

The author would first and foremost like to thank the American Bar Association. It was a pleasure working with them when I wrote the foreword for my father's book, *John Lennon vs. the U.S.A.*, and I appreciate their recognition of the message these cases hold for those attending law school or contemplating a career in the law. Immigration has become a driving force motivating scores of young minds and talent to pursue a career in the field. In this respect, I am grateful to Melanie Leslie and all the prior deans of the Benjamin N. Cardozo School of Law for the trust they placed in my father and me to serve as Adjunct Professors of Law for the last forty-one years, collectively. Having met my wife Amy in my Dad's class and now having two of my four children in my class is a pure joy.

No words can describe the gratitude I have for my father and law partner, Leon Wildes. I have had the good fortune to second seat him my entire professional life. He inspired me to follow in his footsteps. An amazing man of great scholarship and ethics, I cherish the mere task of accompanying him to our offices. I am proud of his legacy and trust. Thanks also to Dad's wife, Alice Wildes, who has shared his life and ours for more than a decade.

I would like to thank our law partner Steven Weinberg and the staff of Wildes & Weinberg, P.C. whose talent and stewardship have helped not only with the matters profiled in this work but have ensured the safety and approval of thousands of immigration clients' cases. With offices in New York City, New Jersey, Florida, and California, we remain available to assist those in need of immigration counsel on business, family, litigation, compliance, and consular immigration matters (see www.wildeslaw. com).

I am most grateful for the love of my wife, Amy Messer Wildes. Her talents as a lawyer are shadowed by her extraordinary judgment and patience. She remains a true partner in everything worthy in my life and most ventures described in this work. Our love to our children Raquel Hailey, Joshua Harlan, Lauren Ruth, Jaclyn Lindsay, and to our newest additions Vicky and Aryeh and their beautiful families.

A special thank-you for the love and support from my brother, Rabbi Mark Wildes, and his wife, Jill, and their children. No doubt our mother, Ruth, though sorely missed, added her own touch to this journey and would be proud of her eight grandchildren and the love and admiration they have for their grandfather. Thank you to my in-laws Susan and Robert Messer for your continued belief and support.

To my good friend David Zedeck, thank you always for your love: believing in me and joining me on this ride. Paul Kemsley (PK) for your wit, graciousness, and love. A special note of thanks is extended to Lawrence Yudess, an accomplished immigration attorney in his own right, for his constant love, support, and Sunday morning conversations. To my mentors, Nick Doria, Larry Schatz, Ben Brafman, and to Harvard Law Professor Alan Dershowitz for their steadfast friendship and scholarship. Through all of their referrals and trust we have fought to safeguard the constitutional underpinnings of our immigration system.

I also thank Yoko Ono Lennon, First Lady Melania Trump, soccer icon Pele, and the many other talents for their trust and friendship. Thank you to Bill McCay, a talented writer, and our agent, John Willig, who worked faithfully to ensure the publication of this most important work.

Foreword

It has been a great honor to be associated with the Wildes family for many years. With Leon, I go back to the days when I was an unknown law teacher, helping him prepare the legal memorandum for John Lennon's immigration case—a case that continues to have far-reaching consequences.

Leon is a great lawyer—probably the greatest immigration lawyer of his generation. Leon helped to establish the field and remains one of its outstanding practitioners. And, as the cases in this book show, his son Michael Wildes has continued to build the family law firm, not just physically but in terms of esteem, prestige, and success.

I've had the pleasure of working with Michael and Leon on several important cases. I don't overstate the fact when I say that the Wildes lawyers are the best. This is not just my belief; it is a conclusion on which I act. When my friends and clients face immigration issues, these are my go-to guys.

In this era of politically motivated immigration ploys and decisions, there are dangerous precedents in drawing lines to exclude people. It's not so long ago that such lines threatened my own family. In the 1930s and 1940s, the march toward the Holocaust set many European Jews in motion, seeking refuge in the United States. Given the economic climate of the time, the United States was unwilling to meet even the restrictive visa quotas available. As the flood of refugees started, the government made the cumbersome immigration process more complicated, more rigorous . . . more exclusionary.

People seeking to come to the United States had to prove they would not become "public charges"—that they had a job waiting for them. My grandfather, Louis Dershowitz, saved twenty-nine of our relatives through the *shul* he'd established in the basement of his Williamsburg home. Using this tiny congregation, he issued letters to fill nonexistent positions for a rabbi, a cantor, and other religious workers to bring endangered family members to this country. These refugees became productive citizens, as have their children and grandchildren.

Although my grandfather might be criticized from a legalistic standard, I believe his actions exemplify the values of what the United States *should* be like. As the cases in *Safe Haven in America: Battles to Open the Golden Door* show, Michael Wildes continues the same struggle—in courtrooms, in the halls of government, and in front of the cameras, fighting for the values to which I hope our country will always remain true.

Alan Dershowitz
New York City, 2018

Preface

"Be safe, son."

How often do fathers use that phrase, and in what circumstances? Certainly, I never expected having to say it as my son, Michael, prepared to go to an unnamed Caribbean destination to meet with a client in the witness protection program of a third country. But perhaps I shouldn't have been surprised. This is the same son who suggested the gift of a bulletproof vest when he began walking a beat with the local auxiliary police. That, I think, is the author of this book in a nutshell.

My professional life was spent representing people before the U.S. Immigration and Naturalization Service, the State Department, and the courts in achieving immigration statuses and defending them against removal. Michael's first position from law school was to work with the U.S. attorney's office in Brooklyn—enforcing immigration law. But when he left government service, he did so with a sense of responsibility. He joined my law firm with an awareness of the blind spots in the system and a determination to help the government—while still protecting his clients and their interests.

To my mind, the most complimentary thing a son can do to honor his father is to model his professional life after his father's. Michael appears to have paid me that ultimate respectful compliment—and he has done so in more than coming aboard at Wildes & Weinberg.

I joined the faculty at Cardozo Law School in 1980, soon after the school opened, to establish the original immigration law course of study. Some thirty years later, I withdrew from the position to concentrate on writing a book on my representation of John Lennon in his deportation case, a story that needed to be told. Michael was immediately hired as adjunct professor to continue teaching the general course on immigration law that I had founded.

However, I can proudly assert that this was not a case of Michael following in my footsteps. He succeeded in broadening our legal practice into areas I had not undertaken, opening offices I had not contemplated. Wildes & Weinberg now maintains a presence in New Jersey, Florida, and California, as well as our New York Office. And as you read the following pages, you will see how he expanded the practice into areas not commonly reached by most immigration lawyers.

Even as a young man, Michael had a highly developed sense of responsibility, which led him to man a beat in Forest Hills, Queens, where we lived. His strong feelings of community responsibility brought him to join Hatzolah, a Jewish volunteer ambulance corps, a connection he has carried on for a quarter of a century, leaving his law office to join an ambulance crew and assist people in need of medical attention when he receives a call. This same sense of responsibility brought him into community work in Englewood, New Jersey, where he served as city councilman and then mayor for nearly a decade.

Also, perhaps rare in a former prosecutor, Michael has a strong belief in second chances. Much of our work involves people who, thanks to a previous brush with the law, find their prospects of achieving immigration status diminished. Like me, Michael believes that a person whose accomplishments can improve our country, whether in the creative world or commerce, should not be barred after paying a just debt to society.

And from John Lennon to Boy George, we have put that principle into action. I hope these ideas will span another generation. Two of Michael's children are already law students at Cardozo and have recently attended his class.

No one should read this book in the expectation of discovering what a typical immigration lawyer does in a typical immigration practice. Michael Wildes is an extraordinary immigration lawyer with a talent for doing the exceptional and accomplishing great things. He has earned and merited the well-deserved success for the highly unusual work depicted in these cases. With such a solid record of capability, I find myself looking to the future with confidence for additional outstanding achievements.

Leon Wildes
New York City, 2018

So Why Write a Book?

If there is a country in the world where concord, according
to common calculation, would be least expected, it is
America. Made up as it is of people from different nations,
accustomed to different forms and habits of government,
speaking different languages, and more different in their
modes of worship, it would appear that the union of such
a people was impracticable; but by the simple operation of
constructing government on the principles of society and
the rights of man, every difficulty retires, and all the parts
are brought into cordial unison.

—*Thomas Paine, Rights of Man*

The law is my profession, but immigration—that seems to be some-
thing that's in my blood. Over the last two decades I've represented both
the government and a wide variety of individuals and corporations in
some of the highest-profile cases in my field. I've represented accused
terrorists, people who fought terrorists, and victims of terrorists. My clients have stretched from government officials seeking asylum to Melania
Trump. I've addressed Congress on immigration and national security
topics, participated in a governor's blue-ribbon advisory panel on immigration in New Jersey, and commented on legal aspects for MSNBC,
CNN, Fox News, CBS, and NBC. As we justly claim on our firm's website, Wildes & Weinberg is one of the best and most preeminent immigration law firms in New York, Florida, New Jersey, and California

Over time, I've seen my chosen line of work undermined by political gridlock, bureaucratic sluggishness, and bitter campaign invective. Stern experience has shown me that there is no such thing as a typical immigration case. But it's also undeniable that a simple bedrock lies beneath every case—dreams. To borrow a concept from tort law, the United States of America is an attractive nuisance, with the hopes of sharing in the American Dream drawing people to these shores, whether it was the hundred or so pilgrims who founded the Plymouth colony, the twelve million people who came through Ellis Island, or the over eleven million illegal entrants today.

The basis of the "American experiment" can be found in the Declaration of Independence: "We hold these truths to be self-evident, that all men are created equal, that they are endowed by their Creator with certain unalienable Rights, that among these are Life, Liberty and the pursuit of Happiness." Those sentiments not only introduced a new nation into the world but induced people from all over the globe to come to the United States and join the experiment. Immigration helped to build the United States into a prosperous, powerful, and stable nation, a safe haven compared to many countries around the globe. More than a million people became naturalized citizens in the last year, and more than 10 percent of the U.S. population are the children of immigrants.

The American Dream, whether of economic advancement, political freedom, or simple personal safety, continues to bring people into our nation, and the body of law covering their admission, how they may become citizens, whether and how long they can reside here, and whether they can or should be deported, has grown into a large and complicated body of scholarship. Practice in the field not only requires knowledge of the applicable statutes but also an understanding of such elements as family law, both here and abroad, criminal law, international law enforcement, espionage and, more recently, terror. Seeking safe haven in the United States continues to bring millions to our country, but the process of finding justice for those "huddled masses yearning to be free" becomes all the more complicated.

In writing *Safe Haven in America: Battles to Open the Golden Door*, I drew on nearly a quarter of a century of my practice in the immigration field. The cases I present, however, don't merely involve legal principles. I wanted to show the human aspects of coming to the United States—the happiness of families and their children, the results of fighting criminality and corruption, the hopes of safely expressing political, religious, or social beliefs and, sometimes, the very stark difference between life and death.

Relating these cases also has a personal dimension. From my immigrant grandfather, my family has practiced the ancient Jewish tradition of *tikkun olam* ("fixing the world" in Hebrew). Helping my clients isn't just a professional obligation; it is a moral and ethical imperative.

The immigrant experience isn't all that far away in my family. My grandfather, Harry Wildes, came from Bialystock, Poland, to become a storekeeper in rural Pennsylvania. My German grandparents were able to migrate successfully to the United States despite the Holocaust. In my various law offices, I've always kept color copies of their German passports, carrying the letter "J" in bright red for "Jew" and the name "Israel" and "Sara" inscribed before and after every male or female name in case somebody had the audacity to erase the "J." Framed next to the passports are letters stating when a German national took my grandfather's paint company, indicating it was *Juden Rein* (purged of Jews), and copies of my grandfather's business documents as he reconstituted himself in the United States.

These documents remind me that however bad situations may become, we've seen worse—and in recent history. I am struck by the portability of my forbears and the significance of being a proud Jew—the biblical people of the passport. They would be very proud to see that their son-in-law and grandson forged a professional life helping others achieve their chosen dreams and a safe haven with the ability to travel and remain permanently in the United States.

I was closest to my maternal grandmother, Hilde Schoenwalter, who until her dying day took extraordinary pride in being a German national, even though she kept those travel documents hidden from view. She felt that I would never make it unless I learned the German language, and despite keeping the winds of war to herself, she took extraordinary pride in her American life. My mother, Ruth, was only one year old when she immigrated to the United States, and her United States citizenship documents sit on my desk every day of my professional life.

My father became one of the earlier pioneers of what has now become a robust and very important field of law in our nation. He produced many early scholarly works on immigration, refugees, and nationality legal issues. He developed a reputation for diligence and for getting approvals of highly sophisticated and complicated matters. In 1970 he was elected national president of the American Immigration Lawyers Association (AILA; previously known as "The American Immigration & Nationality Lawyers," but much to the chagrin of its leadership they did not want to be known as "AINL"). Back then, there were three hundred, maybe four hundred lawyers practicing in the immigration field. Today there are more than 16,000. That alone shows how big the problem of immigration has become.

Thirty years ago our colleagues longed for a time when the old Immigration and Naturalization Service (INS) would be split into two different departments, separating enforcement from adjudication. With creation of the Department of Homeland Security we now have a separate enforcement agency, ICE (Immigration Customs and Enforcement), which has become like a rudderless ship, out of control, with no limitation on its powers as it tramples upon rights and the privacy of citizens and noncitizens alike.

Hard-working new Americans, the backbone of our democracy, are under attack. Anti-immigration voices have been joined by hate groups until it is no longer possible for a candidate to espouse proper immigration laws. The political discourse has deteriorated to a point where candidates for public office are deemed weak on our nation's security if they espouse the virtues of immigrant entrepreneurship. Local legislation is also encouraged to revoke support for "sanctuary cities," and to give local police the power to enforce federal immigration laws. Sanctuary cities have come under attack from the federal level, which has begun withholding needed funds for highway maintenance from cities and states that authorize drivers' licenses for immigrants.

This is not the time to sit idly by while these critical changes are being made that threaten our country. I wrote this book to step beyond the political shibboleths and to find a human dimension to this national problem. If readers draw only that much, I'll count this work a success.

— 1 —

A Star, a Father,
a Legacy

INS has stressed to BUREAU that if LENNON were to be
arrested in US for possession of narcotics he would become
more likely to be immediately deportable.

—*FBI Confidential Memo, July 29, 1972*

Shortly after my father completed his term in office as president
of the AILA, he received a call to consult with former Beatle John Lennon and Yoko Ono Lennon about an immigration matter. The year was
1972. I was eight years old at the time, but even I knew the nation was
involved in a special, historic event—the presidential election that was to
take place that year. Richard Nixon was running for a return to office,
and this would be the first election in which eighteen-year-olds were
permitted to vote.

My father, bless him, was not exactly tuned into the rock music scene.
He had no idea who John and Yoko were when he first met them and, as
he has often related the story, when he returned home to our mother, he
told Ruth about talking with "Jack Lemmon & Yoko Moto."

Even though Dad wasn't so firm on his clients' fame, he understood the facts of the case. John Lennon and his wife Yoko Ono had arrived as visitors in August 1971. The purpose of their trip was to try to locate Yoko's eight-year-old daughter Kyoko, whose father, Tony Cox, had absconded with the child while visiting with her and had whisked her off to parts unknown. Yoko had custody orders from courts in two jurisdictions, and her former husband was held in contempt of those orders.

Lennon, who had a conviction for possession of marijuana, had secured a waiver of his excludability for that visit. The waiver was available only for a temporary admission. There was no waiver whatsoever for permanent residence at that time.

What ensued was a historic abuse of our immigration laws. My father applied for an extension of Lennon's stay for the purpose of helping his wife locate their child. During his time in this country, however, Lennon had made public appearances urging Americans to get out of Vietnam. Inflaming the new eighteen-year-old voters got Lennon on President Nixon's enemies list—and made him a target for dirty tricks.

The president felt he possessed imperial powers and used a slush fund of cash, distributed out of the White House itself, to cover the costs of an undercover group of former government operatives who conducted burglaries, illegal break-ins, and clandestine surveillance operations, some of which involved clearly criminal activity. Richard Nixon believed that if the president authorized such actions, that itself would render them completely legal. He also saw no problem with using the federal immigration system to force Lennon out of the country.

After consulting with the Commission of Immigration, the New York district director told my father that the extension of stay he had requested would be granted for only a month, and that was due only to the long and friendly relationship my father enjoyed with the officials. "Because of you, Leon, but tell your clients to get out of the United States." The Lennons were given a two-week period of time to depart thereafter and, within that two-week period of time the authorization previously given was revoked, and they were declared overstays from the date of revocation. Thus, an entirely phony ground for deportation was set up, along with an "order to show cause."

Moreover, the INS wasn't the only arm of the government used against the Lennons. The FBI conducted continuous surveillance on John and Yoko, and the director, J. Edgar Hoover, reported personally to Richard Nixon's attorney general, his former law partner John Mitchell, with regular accounts of the Lennons' activities. In the face of open surveillance on his clients and wiretaps of his phone calls, my father resorted to discussing the case with my grandfather in Yiddish—at the very least, Dad reasoned, the feds would have to hire a Yiddish speaker to translate.

But there was, unfortunately, very little humor to be found in the situation. The president and his henchmen simply ignored the fact that aliens in the United States had First Amendment rights, which included speaking out against government actions. It took three years of litigation in federal court to secure several documents showing a cover-up and a concerted effort to have the famous Beatle removed for political purposes.

At the time, immigration law prescribed that anyone who was convicted of any offense with respect to narcotic drugs "or marijuana" was both excludable and deportable from the United States with no waiver possible. Accordingly, the government was certain that Lennon would leave because he was not eligible for permanent residence in the United States and that was the only meaningful option he would have in deportation proceedings. In that way, the Nixon administration was convinced that they had put Lennon in an impossible position: he would either leave voluntarily or be deported.

When my father first met the Lennons, John showed my dad his criminal conviction in Britain. The substance he admitted possessing was described as "cannabis resin."

My father asked John, "Was it marijuana?"

"No," John replied, "it was much better than marijuana, cannabis resin is hash." Not only that, but he also stated that the substance had been planted on him by a rogue drug chief at Scotland Yard who had similarly bagged other rock musicians before John's own arrest went down.

John could not explain why his attorney had advised him to plead guilty to an offense he did not commit, so my father became suspicious that the British criminal statute would bear some investigation and research. Finally, Lennon stated that under the British Uniform Rehabilitation of Offenders Act, the conviction would be removed as a matter of law in another year, five years having passed since his conviction.

He had apparently consulted with other immigration lawyers before my father had the privilege of meeting him, and John told him that he understood that he could *never* apply for residence in the United States, although actually being able to live here was a dream of his. Lennon especially loved New York City.

Without any assurances that he would succeed in his efforts, my father indicated that there was a "chance" that John could qualify for permanent residence if his case reached a federal court. Dad also explained to Lennon that if he could show that the substance John was convicted of possessing was not marijuana, he might be successful; also, if British law were such that for some reason John had to be convicted although he was innocent of the charge, that might be useful as well, and ultimately even the statutory commutation of his conviction might be something that could be used in his behalf.

All in, the case was aggressively litigated for five and a half years. Dad lost before the Immigration Service, the Immigration Judge, and then before the Board of Immigration Appeals. But all these legal setbacks were essentially delaying actions while my father unlimbered a new weapon—the Freedom of Information Act (FOIA). This law had only gone into effect in 1967, and Dad made the first use of it in immigration proceedings, going to court to unearth the formerly confidential INS operations instructions on what was called "deferred action"—the use of prosecutorial discretion in trying deportation cases.

My father wielded FOIA as a weapon several times, litigating to look into INS and other government files to prove that members of the Nixon administration had undertaken a selective prosecution to get John Lennon out of the country and then attempted a cover-up of their actions. Dad succeeded in laying bare a conspiracy that apparently began with a note from Senator Strom Thurmond. Passing on information regarding John's antiwar activities, he suggested that "many headaches might be avoided if appropriate action be taken in time." Within days, the machinery started to revoke Lennon's visa status.

Armed with all this new information, Dad was able to prevail in the Court of Appeals—where Chief Judge Irving Kaufman entered a decision in Lennon's favor. The amazing thing about John Lennon is that notwithstanding the pressures placed upon him by the Nixon administration he continued to speak out for the things he believed, including ending the war in Vietnam.

More than forty years have passed since my father won the deportation cases of John Lennon and Yoko Ono Lennon. Their fight against the United States government has become one of the most high-profile and legally important immigration cases in U.S. history. As an immigration attorney myself, I witness both the legacy and the limits of that groundbreaking decision. John and Yoko became two of our nation's most famous immigrants. They were selectively prosecuted for political reasons despite a tremendous outpouring of public support, highlighting their exceptional artistic talent and contributions to our culture. Numerous celebrities testified on their behalf before a courtroom packed with media.

Though stonewalled by the government, my father successfully unearthed the arcane workings of the immigration service. The successful application for "deferred action" that my father filed is heralded today as setting the groundwork for President Obama's Deferred Action for Childhood Arrivals (DACA) program, wherein the president applied the use of prosecutorial discretion to protect from removal those "Dreamers" who had been brought onto American soil by no act of their own.

The Lennons won their battle, but our government continues to enforce many of the same unfair laws and policies that John and Yoko fought against. First, Congress has failed to pass meaningful legislation designed to keep families together. Second, foreigners are still penalized over petty matters committed abroad that would be deemed unconstitutional in the United States. To curtail talented immigrants or refugees cuts against the hospitality and entrepreneurial spirit that our nation was founded upon. From Alexander Hamilton to Albert Einstein, we have benefited from the sheer genius and skills of those "huddled masses" that have come to our shores.

John and Yoko were lucky—and had a great advocate. Let us remember that they were and continue to be two of the most recognizable artists of all time. Yet the government still tried to deport them. History is indeed repeating itself. The pendulum has swung back again to the place it was forty years ago. At this time, we do not have that courageous, noble young dreamer at our side, speaking out against the government's abuse. There is a deafening silence in Congress, and the critical changes needed in our immigration laws are no longer being considered.

I recall meeting the former Beatle at his final immigration hearing. I was twelve years old by then, and it was my brother Mark's ninth birthday when we met the music legend. John was sporting a smile, a new suit, and a fresh green card grasped in his hand after a long, bravely fought legal battle. Our mother brought us to this very important hearing, and it remains a surreal scene etched in my memory: "You can have your father back now," Lennon quipped as all the cameras were focused on him. The case revolutionized immigration law; developed my father's international reputation; and introduced us to a long-standing relationship with the Lennons that continues to this day.

Not many kids from Forest Hills almost had John Lennon at their bar mitzvah—John was invited but had to beg off at the last moment because his young son Sean had an earache. In 1980, barely a week before he was murdered by a mentally unbalanced young man, John sent our family a basket of kosher delicacies with a handwritten note offering his best wishes for the new decade. His passing had a deep effect on our family, and when we lost my mother, Ruth, in 1995, Yoko was quick to offer condolences honoring a long-standing bond of trust and friendship.

In return, my family has always admired John and Yoko as a remarkable pair of human beings. We're not alone in that opinion, of course. The government's deportation attempt unleashed a storm of public protest. You only have to go online to see the myriad videos and efforts that were made to protect John Lennon's ability to remain on U.S. soil. Imagine, if Lennon had been deported, we would have been deprived of his New York City experience, memorialized in his art throughout the remaining years of his life.

Our family forged a deep friendship with John and Yoko, and I still enjoy many referrals thanks to that relationship, not to mention having the privilege of representing Yoko myself over the decades.

— 2 —

What's Past Is Prologue

Like arrows in the hand of a warrior are the children of
one's youth. Blessed is the man who fills his quiver with
them! He shall not be put to shame when he speaks with
his enemies in the gate.

—The Book of Psalms, 127: 3–5

Even as a kid, I was into law and order. At a young age, I devel-
oped a correspondence with the FBI. Long before the *CSI* program
appeared on television, I'd be the one taking fingerprints of my friends
when most would be playing "cops and robbers." I studied the techniques
of the FBI and took plaster casts of footprints, trying to fine-tune my own
detective talents and interests. It was my plan to serve as an FBI agent;
my favorite number was 24, the age required to join.

Growing up in a Sabbath observant Jewish household in Forest Hills,
New York, I was aware of other obligations too. At the tender age of fourteen, I joined the local *Chevra Kadisha* (Jewish burial society). I learned
at a very young age the religious rites and observances in preparing people who passed away for their proper spiritual wash and the donning of
shrouds. My grandfather Max Schoenwalter's best friend Irving Schoen
(who had fled Germany years before) had passed away on a Saturday, and

I was the only one who was able to stand watch and officiate. It is the clearest memory I have of service wherein nobody can say "thank-you," and I learned at a very young age that there were "no pockets in the Kitel" (shrouds). Essentially, at fourteen I learned we would have the privilege to live for a snapshot of time without the ability to take anything with us, and that the legacy of what was important would be memorialized in our deeds.

The law-and-order side of my life emerged again when I took the somewhat unorthodox step (for someone like me) of becoming an auxiliary police officer with the New York Police Department. I had the privilege of donning an NYPD uniform and being introduced to my first bulletproof vest as a gift from my parents. I would walk a beat at the age of eighteen, volunteering my time for ten years in the 112th Police Precinct where I lived. As I went into college and eventually law school, I would often lecture on crime prevention and public safety at local organizations, and I saw firsthand how important it was to help people and properly assess the vulnerability of those in need. Later I would reflect on how that empowered me to take on controversial cases in which justice needed to be served.

In the summer of 1984, I was accepted to be an intern on Capitol Hill for Congressman Gary Ackerman (D-NY). I also joined the late, great Congresswoman Geraldine Ferraro who that summer was selected by Walter Mondale to be the Democratic nominee for vice president of the United States. My time in Washington was a formative experience. I often developed the same spiritual reaction to visiting historical sites in the nation's capital as I do in religious prayer. I never took for granted the liberties and freedoms our founding fathers sought on our shores and the extraordinary sacrifices made by so many to see that the United States remains a safe haven for those at risk and those in need.

Throughout my education, I had the benefit of a warm and loving family. My mother had perhaps the greatest impact on me. I can still hear her shrieks of happiness when I finally passed the bar exam. Immediately, she called my father's receptionist, who in turn shouted: "Ruth in a booth, get Leon on the phone, she has great news!"

Oddly enough, it was my time as a federal prosecutor after I graduated from law school that gave me the greatest insight into immigration law.

From 1989 until 1993, I worked in the Eastern District of New York as a special assistant United States attorney. I am forever indebted to Robert Begleiter and Scott Dunn, two former federal prosecutors who mentored me, trained me as a lawyer, and permitted me to participate in an immigration raid and multiple other prosecutions in Brooklyn. I even participated in a notorious refugee case when the United States attorney for the Eastern District prosecuted Haitians interdicted on international waters.

My service gave me a good sense of the resources the government had available to remove the bad eggs from our shores—and the political nature of this arena. A Cuban national could set foot on dry land and get a green card within a year, whereas a Haitian national could be stopped and taken into custody in international waters. I saw firsthand a system that was not uniform and that discriminated against people based on their national origins. A system of laws that met the economic needs for one generation but had a patchwork of bandages to address modern challenges rather than uniformly setting standards to protect our homeland and ensure that the greatest entrepreneurs and risk-takers found a home in America's corridors of business. My time as a federal prosecutor representing the United States government and its many agencies (United States Army, FBI, etc.) afforded me with an opportunity to develop my own sea legs and to not be intimidated by our government's reach and resources.

Also around this time, in 1991, I joined Hatzolah, a volunteer ambulance service in the New York area. It was right before my daughter Raquel was born. She was the first girl in our family, and I was concerned because she did not come with any instruction booklet. I figured it was best that I learn firsthand how to protect her, if needed. For the past twenty-five years, I've remained a certified emergency medical technician (EMT) in New York State, often going on calls during work hours, evenings, and weekends to help complete strangers. I've always kept in mind that I'll be judged by what my children see and not what I say.

At last, I came to join Wildes & Weinberg, P.C., the firm my father had founded. Following in Dad's footsteps was my destiny. Most kids grew up wanting to be a fireman or policeman—I certainly had a flirtation with that. My father, by inspiring me through his exemplary character and friendship, convinced me that this path came closest to those life-saving services. On any given Sunday when I was young, we would go to the office. There I would spend hours cutting scrap paper, interrupted by an outing to a nearby waterfall park at Fifty-third and Madison, where Dad and I would dine on kosher sandwiches my mother had packed for us. We've been paying rent at 515 Madison Avenue for the fifty-three years that I have been fortunate to be alive. My Dad's work ethic and success paved the way ultimately for me to manage his practice, but it was his diligence and scholarship that inspired me to become a lawyer.

Let me make it plain—my connection with my father's office didn't end when my paper-cutting days were over. I went to college two days a week (from 8 a.m. until 8 p.m.) and worked the remaining three days in Dad's practice. This gave me a chance to come up through the ranks, often sleeping outside overnight for a few bucks so I could get on line for an early appointment at the federal building downtown for our clients.

After one sleepless night (and being solicited by prostitutes while waiting on the line), I remember meeting Paloma Picasso as my father accompanied her to her green card interview. Some years later, when she decided to abandon her lawful permanent residence, I accompanied her myself to the immigration offices. What a treat it was to see some of the private artwork that her notorious father, Pablo Picasso, had painted for her before I took her downtown.

All these experiences amounted to a private tutelage in addition to my formal legal training. By the time I sat down with my own clients, I already had a good sense that these individuals were not just paperwork. They were part of a magnificent, tremendously important journey like the one that brought my family to America. To this day, each story remains a sacred trust.

My commitment to public service shouldn't be a surprise, having worked on Capitol Hill, studied the law, and put in a stint as a prosecutor. My slogan for the many campaigns that I ran for city council and ultimately mayor of Englewood, New Jersey, was "Public Service. Public Trust." In 2004, I became the thirty-sixth mayor of the city where my wife Amy and I live, and I found myself thrust into a remarkable vantage point for appreciating my life as an immigration lawyer. The New Jersey League of Municipalities entrusted me with the position of chairman for its Immigration Task Force. I had the privilege of traveling the state, meeting with counterpart mayors, and participating in local and international mayors' conferences.

From a policy viewpoint, however, the situation was depressing. While presidents and Congress left our immigration laws dormant, our nation's cities saw an influx of immigration and suffered its collateral consequences. Muster zones with day laborers filled our nation's streets. Stacking conditions developed in our cities—residential corridors where illegal tenancies were created by landlords, forcing people to live in precarious conditions. I met with families who lost loved ones and first responders who were put in harm's way by the gross inaction of our federal officials in Washington.

At the same time, I often spent weekends marrying couples, and welcoming their families into my Sabbath home so my children would encounter love in all shapes, sizes, and the magnificence of the diversity to which I was exposed. They would see an African American couple jumping over a broom in my living room, which was customary in the days of slavery when there was no officiant, and others taking photos of my grandparents' passports neatly framed in my household as well. My children appreciated their heritage as they saw others revel in their own.

In many ways, a lot of the different worlds that I had lived in came together when I was wrapping up my second term as mayor in 2009. This is when Libyan dictator Muammar Gaddafi threatened to sleep within our city environs. Gaddafi succeeded in pitching a tent and sleeping in Paris, only to be denied by Mayor Bloomberg in New York City when the Libyan leader wanted to do the same in Central Park. This was the dictator's flamboyant way of traveling. Bloomberg said no, and then Gaddafi sought to sleep on a property owned by his government within the City of Englewood.

Also at this time, Gaddafi extended a warm welcome to the recently released Lockerbie bomber Abdelbaset al-Megrahi on his return to Libya. That event, and Gaddafi's planned trip to New York to attend a United Nations General Assembly, offended many—the dictator embraced al-Megrahi publicly in the wake of the 9/11 attacks. Some 259 people died as a result of the 1988 bombing of Pan Am Flight 103 over the Scottish town of Lockerbie, and thirty-three of them had hailed from New Jersey.

I found it offensive that Gaddafi offered a hero's welcome to a con-victed terrorist. I was infuriated and publicly stated that our community would not forget his acts of terrorism nor pitch a white tent and red carpet for the Libyan dictator. For years his government had not paid a nickel of property taxes, and my police department was required to protect the location and our public works to remove their rubbish without fee. The property that he intended for his temporary residence received visits from agents of the Secret Service and the close protection division of the State Department. The property itself had been in a state of disrepair for many years, but in recent months the Libyans began to renovate it. Together with my code enforcement officials and some fancy footwork in Bergen County Superior Court, we were able to stop the construction, and Gaddafi was forced to move on to find other sleeping arrangements.

Ultimately the dictator was forced to sleep at a United Nations facil-ity. The State Department was upset and concerned to protect its own political interest in other countries, but I could not for the life of me imagine giving the progenitor of modern-day terrorism a good night's sleep and safe haven. I went on British television and stated proudly, "I am an American and a Jew, and I will not forget the souls lost from my home state."

I stood firm despite all the negative press Gaddafi ultimately hired (not to mention the thousands of disciples of Louis Farrakhan and the Nation of Islam, who staged a major rally outside the United Nations to show their love and support). I have to admit, though, that my police chief felt it wise for the city's Jewish mayor to receive twenty-four-hour close protection by Englewood's finest. Despite all the brouhaha, I don't regret it. This event resonated and hit a cord in my family's DNA.

Another strand in the tapestry of my life is education. I have had the privilege now of teaching immigration law as an adjunct professor at the Benjamin N. Cardozo School of Law for nearly a decade. I had good preparation—my father taught the same class for more than thirty-three years. Having sat through his class prep as well as attending and tap-ing many of his class sessions was an excellent foundation for my own professional life. To this day, one of my greatest exercises is learning the immigrant story of each of my law students and developing a relationship with them during the course of a semester. I spend many days mentoring my students, advising them that 95 percent of their practice will evolve as an iceberg, below eye level view.

The best talents in our field remain those who are affected personally by their own family's narrative and journey to this great nation. As the law evolves, the one common denominator that binds many of the professionals in this arena are the beautiful stories and the efforts families have made to settle on our shores. What follows are some of my more memorable ones.

"What Color Is Your Green Card?" A "Typical" Immigration Case (and Why There Is No Such Thing)

Having a Green Card (officially known as a
Permanent Resident Card) allows you to live and work
permanently in the United States. The steps you must take
to apply for a Green Card will vary depending on your
individual situation.

—*U.S. Citizenship and Immigration Services*

Green cards have actually gone through many colors over the decades! As with so much in the immigration field, there is a great deal more than meets the eye. One of the most important things for an immigration attorney to learn is the ability to discern when a "routine" immigration case will turn out not to be routine at all. Look at my father's most famous case—filing a simple extension of stay turned into a five-and-a-half-year struggle with the federal government. Whether it is a business person coming to the United States with a visa need or a high-asset intelligence opportunity for our government's military and security community, nothing is ever "business as usual."

Every immigration case is unique. Of course, many of the cases are administrative in nature and repeat themselves, but each case that comes into my office requires a personal intake (although these days we handle them by Skype and telephone as well). With search engine optimization and social media turning so much of people's lives into public information these days, it's a professional must to evaluate all the available facts of a client's journey and not make any assumptions. Many of our younger associates are critical that we still use the intake sheet that my father devised in the 1960s, but it's an invaluable tool for organizing the necessary information.

Clients often encounter our immigration system through employment, familial relationships, or investing in an enterprise that will benefit the U.S. economy. Despite the route, each client is unique and needs to substantiate his or her eligibility for a status. I recall sitting with my father for months when I began practicing as a lawyer, watching him with extraordinary patience repeat himself to make sure the client understood what was going on. He would amaze me with his ability to place himself in the client's shoes. To this date, when a client calls the office, Dad often takes notes from that initial call, following a system he devised to memorialize all the details so that nothing is lost. "New Matter" calls are immediately taken or responded to.

A memo is still dictated by a partner in front of a client. We want to make sure the client understands the operational facts and legal eligibility for a particular visa or remedy before the immigration court. For marketing purposes, the first line often finds us citing who referred the matter and the last line the individual's cell phone and email for follow up purposes. Most important, we are transparent regarding the likelihood of success and the financial obligations so from the onboarding of a matter a client is satisfied that there is a written record of expectations as well.

A typical client would be given a one-hour period of time to see a senior professional or partner. Ethical proprieties require lawyers to protect clients' secrets. Capable language proficiency for legal professionals helps to gather and elucidate salient facts at that first meeting, which can take place in one of our many offices and on occasion in foreign countries.

Being a good listener and knowing the law go hand in hand. Many clients are shopping for a second opinion of another professional's counsel. Most clients are capable of drawing conclusions very quickly. I strategically station people outside my office who can help with some of the administrative needs, or undertake quick research as needed, so that we can move matters along with a professional cadence and expectation.

I prefer to have three professionals on the team (a lawyer and a paralegal or two lawyers in addition to me). Clients are given instructions to make sure that all members of the team are copied on emails, and each individual's responsibility is clearly delineated so there are redundancies in place in the event a client has an emergency and needs to communicate immediately.

To set the context of our law practice, it is useful to note the five major areas for which my firm is known:

1. Business Immigration Law Practice (I teach business immigration law at the Cardozo School of Law). Here we deal with all the business visas that individuals seek in order to work, invest, or develop their wares in the United States.
2. Family Immigration Law Practice. Here we deal with individuals marrying American citizens or permanent residents and families being reunited on U.S. soil.
3. Compliance Unit. Here we toil with the onboarding of citizens and noncitizens into the U.S. workforce (Form I-9 compliance audit, etc.).
4. Litigation. We have a robust litigation group and offer representation both in federal court and for removal proceedings before immigration judges. Our talented asylum unit enjoys a reputation for successfully achieving political asylum for scores of clients both administratively and in the courts.

5. Foreign Consular Process. We deal with the many United States embassies the world over.

At business networking groups, I quip that a good lead in our practice would be "anybody with an accent." With offices in New York, New Jersey, Florida, and "by appointment only" in California, we are dedicated to the exclusive practice of United States immigration and nationality law—and business is good.

Historically, the United States has prided itself on being a nation built by immigrants, and it remains a magnet to the world's cultures. Industry leaders continually seek prospective talented immigrants from nations throughout the world, a practice that our firm expanded to include representation of U.S. firms anxious to attract people with needed skills. We counsel local and international companies with regard to all aspects of business-related immigration law. Our clients include Fortune 500 companies, universities, financial interests, shipping, hospitality, and not-for-profit institutions. We also represent individuals who wish to work in the United States, including foreign students hoping to join our workforce for their first job after graduation.

We provide guidance on complex immigration issues in virtually every visa category and are privileged to represent individuals who, because of their extraordinary ability in their field or because of their substantial investments in the U.S. economy, do not require corporate sponsorship to immigrate. Each day we advise our clients about the best short- and long-term visa strategies for their specific needs. We counsel them on a wide variety of business and family visas.

Dealing as we do with such a wide array of interests, we have learned there is no such thing as a typical client. We have no idea on any given day whether a rock star or a housekeeper is going to walk into our office. Either way the ethical practices that my father taught me make one thing clear—you could not tell the difference by the way I act to either. Early in my career I saw and understood from my father's practice that it was important for us to create a culture in the office that conveyed to clients in very short order that we appreciate that this is not just a case, but a journey that they are taking and we are meritorious ourselves for being chosen to play a role in their lives. Thus, it's important for me to understand that as much as somebody is coming to see me, I have a limited window of time to convey this properly to our clients.

It is difficult to maintain the trust of clients when you receive hundreds of emails a day on several servers and iPhones, meeting and talking to hundreds of people in the course of a week. Creating a culture of honesty and transparency is critical. This is especially true when we deal with couples coming into the system because of marriage to an American citizen. People in these unions receive only conditional permanent residence if their marriage has lasted less than two years. The government simply does not trust the institution of marriage—it has been abused as a shortcut to a green card by too many. Thus newlyweds are subject to extra scrutiny, and as lawyers we find ourselves embroiled in the drama of our clients' relationships. If the proverbial dishes start flying in the household months after we filed a case, we have to know—and know how to deal with it.

I had the privilege of marrying many couples when I was mayor, but I am selective as to which wedded pairs I can ethically represent. The husband and wife must establish themselves as a bona fide couple, even to the use of social media such as Facebook and other options on the Internet. I have learned that it's an interesting balancing act—exhaustively ascertaining the facts of a relationship while also respecting the privacy of our clients and obtaining permission to discuss our representation publicly.

The way you comport yourself to your staff must be equally dignified as you present yourself to a client and, being clear in expectations, whether in writing or otherwise, is important. I insist that calls are returned the very same day we receive them. We do not ever criticize a client because the client showed up without an appointment, and we offer more value by not billing them by the hour but by encouraging them to call and email us so that we meet their needs, satisfy their curiosity, and allay their apprehensions. Clients who are entrepreneurial in spirit will feel this energy and passion in the way we express ourselves but will move on from our offices if they are not convinced we are sincere.

Quality work, favorable adjudications, and stellar communications with our clients are paramount. We make a specific point to reinforce the fact that clients are not just names on a list, or dollar signs—they are people with families, goals, and ambitions who have entrusted us to perform a vital service, the success of which will change their lives. Not only gaining but maintaining the trust throughout (and after) representation is a driving force that has kept our practice alive for nearly sixty years.

Client service means not just good service but superlative service. Happy clients are easy clients to work with, deal with, and get paid from, with the least number of headaches. In the end, the biggest asset we have is our reputation. Controlling client expectations is significant; we never promise more than we can deliver but deliver more than what we promised.

Another critical part of the equation is communication. Even if we don't have something for the client to sign, we try to keep in touch. We learn that it doesn't pay to "go dark" on clients and wait for them to contact us. Emails make this process much easier. Yet you would be surprised how many firms let clients languish, even ignoring direct requests.

Our firm is a family affair, with me following in my father's footsteps. It's a responsibility—I have to be available 24/7. My staff is always watching: How do I speak to my family? How flexible am I? How do I handle personal challenges? With such an open relationship, I am not embarrassed to apologize for mistakes that I make, and I pride myself on being able to accept the same in kind.

Hand in hand with this is accessibility: almost every morning, the first hour of my day is spent in as many as four coffee meetings with students I'm mentoring, vendors supplying professional services, and lawyers looking for work. I try to relate to each of my clients on a personal basis, being honest about my own shortcomings and trying to learn what motivates them. Some people come to me for counsel while dealing with personal tragedy on top of what seems an insurmountable challenge with the immigration authorities. I try to be sensitive and discreet when I discuss such matters on the telephone or communicate to them in emails. I've been known to introduce a helpful client to another with similar interests. Casual gestures—such as personal notes and small gifts—have a place in developing a stronger friendship with people I represent.

Clients will refer you as an individual, not just a business professional. Hence, your personal life can be just as powerful as your professional life, and activities outside the office can have serious consequences for your professional life. Considering how quickly people can post and tag pictures online, and the wildfire speed technology gives to rumors and gossip, it's important to be wary of one's surroundings both in and out of the office. Confidentiality and discretion are critical. Whether you speak to somebody through writing or in person, all professionals must earn a reputation for being discreet. You can lose ground and clients by not protecting someone's privacy. You must discipline yourself and act responsibly even if your client does not.

On a personal rather than professional level, I have to be thankful for my good health and what I call my "portability." I need to be ready and mobile to respond to a client's call, even if that means an international public or private flight. If I don't show up for the opportunity to represent somebody, I can be sure someone else will. Given these circumstances, I'm very lucky that I "married up" and chose a spouse wisely. I had the good fortune of meeting my wife Amy in law school, where we both attended my father's immigration law class together. In our family circle, the law firm is considered to be one of our "children." Amy has always encouraged me be available at all times for my clients and traveled internationally with me and my father when necessary.

I will never forget a phone call I received from a client after I had joined my daughter Raquel in her "midnight run" at the Ramaz High School in Manhattan. (This was a program where we were giving out food and clothing to those in need on the streets.) The client, Paul Kemsley, a British entrepreneur, called my mobile phone stating, "wheels up at Teterboro in sixty minutes, dinner with soccer legend Pele in Switzerland tomorrow night." Now this would not have happened if my client had not had my cell phone (my mobile telephone number is actually printed on my business card); had he not wanted me to be there at that pivotal moment in time; and had my wife and daughter not allowed me to take off!

If there is one main ingredient for all cases, it is making sure we are up on the scholarship, improving ourselves, and mentoring others. I learn more about the law by teaching students and have increased my own personal knowledge by engaging in the research and findings of our clients' cases. This includes drafting articles, putting myself out for public debate, and commenting in public media as well.

Much has changed in our practice over the years. At one point we represented most, if not all, of the major Canadian, Swiss, German, and European banks, who were moving their personnel into the United States. As the economy thinned and firms took matters in-house, we built a new business model in our practice. With many staff accommodating a single financial institution, we realized that we would end up in a precarious circumstance if our clients went elsewhere or decided to handle their visa work in-house. Simply put, if revenues of our clients and their profits were down, we were going to see less immigration traffic to the United States from our own clients. Hence, it was important for us to build up the litigation practice and family ledger so we would have consistent traffic. I sought to further expand our portfolio of clients and litigation so that we now enjoy a robust following in the world of fashion, art, sports, and entertainment, including hospitality. I often find myself attending trade conferences in the food, restaurant, and beverage industry; providing copy for articles in trade publications; and traveling the world over to enhance our portfolio in areas of industry that are not typically represented in the region where we practice.

My search for clients has reinforced what many studies have already found—immigrants remain the greatest risk-takers and entrepreneurs, bringing an extraordinary work ethic as they endeavor to help make a fresh start or protect themselves from harm's way. Many immigrants are solo business owners out of necessity. They would rather be responsible for themselves and employ others, or they realize they are better off working for themselves. I am impressed by immigrant business owners who do not have university degrees and often excel in the professional world. They do not rely on a piece of paper to succeed but use their own creativity and innovation in a competitive economy.

Having chosen us as counsel, what can a client expect? Again, there is no routine answer. The shelf life of an immigration case could range from a few weeks to a decade. Conventionally, clients first present us with temporary visas and often face personal or professional changes or challenges in their professional lives that require commensurate visa requests. Many are forced to make new applications, apply for extension requests, or adjust their status to permanent residence. The good news is that most applications end ultimately in the coveted United States citizenship.

Immigration and Anti-Terrorism

If asked to answer the question of what has created the greatest impact in the immigration field during my career, I would not respond with a piece of legislation, a president's executive action, or a court case. My answer would be the events of September 11, 2001. Two buildings, 220 stories in all, burned and collapsed as our nation looked on in horror. Smoldering gray air drifted past the Statute of Liberty. I was there the day after with an ambulance crew that I volunteer with, a few thousand feet away from Ground Zero on the bucket brigade. Americans knew now that they lived in a different world—one that was forever changed.

By sunset on that very day, few people could deny that the United States now faced an extraordinary crisis. Immediately a number of voices rose, attempting to conflate terrorism with immigration. The U.S. Department of Justice recently released a report with this alarming headline: almost three-quarters of those convicted for international terrorist events since 9/11 were immigrants—402 out of 549 individuals. The report, however, ignores some 1,400 incidents of domestic terrorism perpetrated by all-American extremists. Interestingly, given the concurrent battle over the administration's travel ban, the Justice Department failed to link the immigrant terrorists with banned countries—because there's little evidence of violence from immigrants from any of those nations.

Yes, the evil of any terrorist's act does not necessarily reflect his nationality—as American terrorist Timothy McVeigh illustrated all too well. However, by challenging innocent Muslims in our country, we only add to the heartbreak of the growing body count internationally. Still, September 11 must mark a major shift felt in the United States. We can no longer indiscriminately hold ourselves out as a beacon of freedom to the world if it means compromising our safety.

Many of us believe that this war actually began in 1979 when our hostages were taken in Iran. September 11 was merely the first suicide attack of magnitude on United States soil. I testified in 1999 on Capitol Hill and talked about a score of cases, underlining the importance of cultivating intelligence and the imperative of responding in a measured sense to terrorism. By debating the propriety of Homeland Security and turning our back on scores of immigrants, we have allowed terrorist cells to grow over time and even to strengthen. We cannot resort to extremism to find them or to cull them out. Common sense dictates that until we ascertain that we are again reasonably secure, we cannot fully give the benefit of our rights to aliens who present even the slightest potential threat to us, nor should we be politically correct with a figurative gun held to our head.

For the longest time there were no departure controls, and we had many perpetrators of terrorism within our own grip, only to see them leave and return unfettered across our porous borders. In employing our immigration laws to combat terrorism, the United States cannot be bound by the same blindfold that the rest of our justice system uses for fair judgment. It makes a mockery of our constitution to extend the rights to aliens who may cause a serious threat to the very Americans who fought to protect them. It is very important that we rise to this challenge while maintaining our role as the world's moral compass, a nation that takes great pride in a history of success built on the backbone of immigrant Americans.

As an immigration lawyer who has dealt with terrorists and defectors, I've seen the opportunities for our government to acquire crucial human asset intelligence. I have flown to the corners of the world and worked to utilize immigration law as a tool to battle that elusive enemy, the terrorist. There is a delicacy when handling any matter for a client who is embroiled in the world of anti-terrorism. For years we've represented power companies, former diplomats, and scores of businessmen and women who had access to intelligence that was not readily available to law enforcement and our intelligence services. The governing rules, however, have always remained the same: to be transparent and ethical while maintaining a sense of vigilance and immediacy at all times.

Many of these cases required thinking outside of the box, such as hiring translators and swapping them out frequently so no one could gather intelligence, thus protecting my client's privacy to a greater degree than normal. Being able to secrete a client in a hotel, arrange for close protection, or jump on an airplane on a few hours' notice has proven critical. Even the dictation of memorandums and discreet administrative support were decided in the best interest of our client's privacy and the safety of their intelligence information.

Our office has been approached by agents from many federal agencies and intelligence services through the years, seeking our support. Often they were frustrated by bureaucratic obstacles that limited their efforts to secure human asset intelligence. Our own experience was a learning curve. Maintaining the confidentiality of our client secrets and respecting the attorney-client privilege while concurrently managing the government and an inquisitive media took talent and time to perfect. There is nothing routine about getting a fee agreement from a goat herder who saved a Navy SEAL or drafting an asylum claim for a Saudi diplomat who was fearful that he would be gunned down on a public street. Each required my best team and a tailored response based on a sound legal strategy.

The proximity of our office to the United Nations, local police precinct, and safe retreat hotels for impromptu meetings allowed us to pivot to protect our clients and advance their interests. Adaptability, initiative, and tenacity has protected the lives of many of our clients, from simple tasks such as ensuring that they have privacy where needed (often we bring clients through a nondescript entrance to our building to avoid videotaping) to ensuring that they cooperate with law enforcement in a transparent, unfettered fashion.

One of the constants in my professional life has been listening to my father speak in the same tone and temperament to my mother, rest her soul, clients, and other loved ones. I could never tell if he was speaking to a millionaire or a day laborer. Today's modern heroes and cooperators in the fight against terror are all individuals who breathe the same air and deserve the same dignity and time. In this respect, I am grateful for the trust that our law enforcement and intelligence community has placed in us.

There was a time when it would have been inappropriate for an FBI agent or intelligence officer to refer a legal matter to a lawyer. Things have evolved, and now we are engaged by their legal counsel or summoned for inquiries by agents in the field who have immediate needs for immigration counsel. Even the federal government and its agents have been frustrated by some of the bureaucratic backlog and the politics of immigration when human asset intelligence has played heavily in our nation's interests.

There are cases that I am not permitted to discuss without breaching commitments I made and threatening the lives of very important cooperators. I have a letter from the Central Intelligence Agency giving me unfettered access to a file that I handled years ago—but which I was not permitted to maintain in my office because of the delicacy of our client's engagement with the U.S. intelligence community. In fact, at the time, agents came to my office with encryption devices, taking my client's statement and having me review the contents in a secure fashion to avoid any exposure or breach of their methods and procedures. For a few other matters, I was given an index card with a conversion of letters to numbers so I could send encoded telefaxes to a government agent and set meeting places as needed.

There was certainly nothing routine about requests I received on the Sabbath when it came to our nation's security. Often I would find myself speaking to one or two rabbis in confidence about the required tasks and whether or not a breach of religious law would be permitted given the high stakes. On one occasion, I had to drive to meet two naval intelligence agents for a former Saudi diplomat during the Rosh Hashanah holiday after the USS *Cole* had been attacked to affect a proper consultation. I was warned how to sit in restaurants, confer with clients in private, and what personal safety measures to take both in my offices and residences. To this date I sit in a restaurant facing the main entrance and often cut a meeting short to change locations if I am not comfortable. The taping of conversations, listening devices, and sweeping for same seems routine in many of the matters I am engaged in for both my client's and my own protection. I am particularly sensitive when approached by foreign ambassadors and the witness protection services of other nations when they seek safe haven for a rogue individual on U.S. soil. Matters of confidentiality vary from state to state, and often I consult with criminal counsel so I am prepared to protect all of my client's legal interests.

On many of our high-profile defection and whistle-blower cases, we depend on the glare of media coverage to protect our clients' lives, given the politics of a particular region or the hesitancy of our government to act due to delicate diplomatic considerations. We have developed a specialty, learning to pace the media to effectuate a protracted campaign on behalf of our clients. If the FBI was not going to protect a Saudi diplomat or a religious cleric who remained imperiled for coming forward, we were going to see that the continued position in the public eye would keep that individual healthy and alive. Often the front-page reporters of major newspapers called me looking for a scoop on a matter I was handling or to inquire whether a certain defector was heading my way. Negotiating the exact photo and the impression that the caption would have on my client's adversaries was much more than a mere writing job. Often the world's finest journalists (some who died in the field) covering the world's hottest topics reach out to us, pitching coverage that would be the only shield we would have on a matter. As a New Yorker, I likened it to the lights being turned on—making all the roaches run for cover.

Over the years, we've become quite proficient in the use of the media as a highly effective legal tool. However, when a client is concerned about privacy or is concerned about the backlash of a public rendition of their case, we stand down. On many occasions the only pressure that can be brought to bear is by engaging the media. I feel frustrated when clients hesitate or make disclosures in a haphazard way that does not help their case. Developing a reporter's trust is significant because they vet the authenticity and credibility of a client's claims.

Although the world has changed in recent years, the immigration authority has not. The paperwork reduction act has reduced a one-page "Notice of Appearance of Attorney" to a four-page document. Many well-intended government officers and agents are incapable of reaching humanitarian conclusions and favorable dispositions, given conflicting policies from new presidents and outdated immigration laws promulgated and rendered stale as economic metrics evolved. As a result, clients shop for a favorable venue or find themselves facing removal from the United States despite not having engaged in criminality due to running afoul of technical breaches. Even inadvertent trips and international travel during the pendency of an application for permanent residence without proper permission could render invalid an application for permanent residence. Such an individual could be barred from returning to the United States. Even those who have been vetted for criminality can be deemed inadmissible if they concede any relevant element of a charge at a point of entry into the United States or before any domestic immigration official. Simple departures from or entries into the United States are no longer a routine matter. Often our staff have to prepare individuals on weekends and in evening hours in anticipation of their urgent impromptu travels.

Whatever the sphere—business, personal, or security-related—nothing is routine.

— 4 —

The Glare of the Spotlight and Its Dark Side

Without publicity there can be no public support, and without public support every nation must decay.

—*Benjamin Disraeli*

Too bad there's not a law school class on media management. From the early days of my career, I learned this skill on the job. When I was a young federal prosecutor, the offices were going to have their annual celebratory holiday party at a location under federal prosecution. I was given the delicate task of handling the matter. In the private realm, the media is often readily available but can become troublesome if you do not control it. There are ethical considerations with regard to clients' privacy. Technological concerns also enter into the equation—as the world of social media evolved so did my use of it.

My firm has represented stars from the rock music, theater, and sports worlds—clients who are used to the public spotlight and know how to deal with it. As I embark on my third decade in the practice of law, I find my interest and sympathies most stirred by the noncelebrities whose conduct or circumstances require the sword of public opinion to cut through legal obstacles: the spouses of those who fell on September 11, 2001, at the World Trade Center; women whose husbands absconded with their children; or young foreigners who stepped up with natural acts of heroism, instinctively and without hesitation. It doesn't take a seasoned journalist to see that people like these deserve a spot over the fold on a newspaper's front page or a mention on the evening news. They only need one look at someone like Deena Gilbey, whose husband helped scores of people safely out of the World Trade Center, only to perish himself at that very site.

Getting to a point where a lawyer can confidently articulate a client's plight and stand in strong stead while in debate against a talk show host is a journey. My apprenticeship in this art began in 1995; I appeared on scores of televised interviews for news organization (such as Fox News) that had offices in New York at that time but didn't even broadcast into the New York City region. In many ways, I love the work that I do, imagining my client's narrative being broadcast and the experience shared by viewers, listeners, or readers. Such publicity can effect change not only for the client but for scores of others who are often in the same peril.

It is easy to get a visa if you are Pele, a Miss Universe, Chef Jean-Georges, or a noted scholar in your field. However, my greatest satisfaction derives from cases of everyday individuals who are faced with a challenge and the way they step up to meet it. Often it is more impressive for me to sit with day laborers than to sit on a private plane with a celebrity. The most delicate cases involve clients who must deal with a medical emergency while concurrently facing federal prosecution by the immigration authorities.

I was away at Mount Airy Lodge in the Poconos for Passover in April 2001 when a long-standing case in our office became acute. Mariann LaMonte-Shaban and her husband, Louis, were asking immigration not to deport Louis to South Africa. It was difficult enough for the young couple, confronted with challenges, but then Mariann was diagnosed with cancer. The INS wanted to deport Louis, who was thirty-six years old, because he overstayed his tourist visa for a two-week period of time in 1994. Our response was to rally our senators to the couple's cause while getting in front of cameras to explain that, despite his inadvertence, my client was not a criminal and did nothing more than fall in love with an American citizen who took ill.

I encountered a similar but even more heartbreaking case when I met Mamadou Soumare, a cab driver from Mali who similarly overstayed a visa and returned home from a long evening's work to discover that his wife and four daughters had been killed in a fire. He had an angelic presence about him and wanted desperately to bury his family in Mali, but the INS would not permit him to come back into the United States. I took to the airwaves to publicize Mamadou's case, including "The O'Reilly Factor" on Fox News. Bill O'Reilly is a tough interviewer, but I managed to convince him that we should change our immigration laws and allow the dead to be buried, considering the circumstance behind this tragedy. In both cases, the federal government seemed blind to the catastrophic events that befell these individuals. Still worse, the bureaucracy was incapable of immediately rendering a favorable and supportive result.

The same feeling evolved as I represented several World Trade Center surviving spouses who lost loved ones on September 11. One of these bereft families had the tragedy compounded; en route to the World Trade Center site, a collision with a National Guard vehicle sent military-style steel tent poles flying into their truck, killing several additional family members. I could not understand how a country that established itself as a safe haven for liberty and justice did not have a flexible immigration law that would allow a person to mourn, focusing on loved ones and "next steps" rather than having them dropped into a tailspin, literally fighting for the right to remain while reeling from emotional and sometimes physical pain.

No school or mentor ever prepared me for the roles I have found myself playing in order to stand in solidarity with my clients, often stepping into their shoes and expressing myself when they could not. I remember my wife and I traveling to Washington to stand on the steps of the Capitol building with Pat Roush, whose daughters were absconded by her husband. Photographers and news cameras recorded us holding up her children's U.S. citizen passports, pleading that our leaders not forget two young souls while they bartered billions of dollars of business with an ally that did not sign the Hague Convention.

If fame is brief, media fame can be even more fleeting, and for many bureaucrats, invisible. When I represent a noncitizen who acted bravely in a crisis, I am astonished to find that individual being penalized by our immigration authorities. Yet, surprisingly, we often receive help from people within the government. Special agents of the many intelligence and law enforcement agencies that I have the privilege to deal with will take action without fanfare to facilitate information and resources where needed. Many government operatives dipped into their own pockets to hand a client money to travel to safety, and others have advised us of the political entanglements we face.

During my term as mayor of Englewood, New Jersey (D, 2004–2010), one of my most cherished perks was the chance to bring individuals whose meritorious conduct deserved recognition into our public schools. I could think of no better opportunity than the chance for students of my community to meet "real heroes." My client Kwame James, who subdued Richard Reid, the infamous "shoe bomber," enthralled a packed audience by discussing eight keys points that prepared him to save several hundred lives and millions of dollars worth of airplane when he subdued the would-be terrorist. Though he consistently downplays his actions, James remains a true hero who acted instinctively and deserves celebrity status.

Even people who are used to the red carpet can find themselves going through painful situations and understand how the use of a little star power can help in stirring public awareness and sympathy so that others will not have to endure the same plight. I was approached by Harvard Law Professor Alan Dershowitz to help represent noted actress Kelly Rutherford, whose children had been effectively deported due to a poor decision by a state court judge in a divorce proceeding. We stood before a federal judge and a large media contingent to see that this would not happen to others.

Not every case demands media attention, nor does every client's interest gain stronger ground with widespread coverage. Whatever the correct course may be, the first step is to evaluate whether or not reporters have already covered the story. Second, I would evaluate whether a print campaign would be the most effective approach, with an eye to whether it could eventually lead to an even more effective network television media campaign.

On most occasions, it is my practice to get "sign offs" from clients in writing to clarify the benefits of going public and to prevent misunderstandings. In many instances, I warned clients that I would not continue to participate in their matter if they sought the attention of a foreign journalist. In matters as delicate as attempted defections, there's always the danger that a "journalist" may also be a foreign agent. On the other hand, I fondly recall meeting on many occasions with acclaimed journalist personalities who often faced peril to get an important story. Marie Colvin would call me years after my handling of Mohammed Khilewi's defection, and I developed a very close relationship with Geraldo Rivera, who not only played a heroic role in reporting from war-torn parts of the world but remains a dear friend and has referred others in jeopardy to our firm.

I will never forget standing with New York Senator Al D'Amato against the backdrop of Lady Liberty herself in New York Harbor to publicize the plight of twenty-nine flight attendants from Delta Airlines. These employees were told by immigration that their visas were mistakenly issued and that they needed to return to Poland. The senator suggested we co-host a joint press conference on historic Liberty Island. It was the Friday after Thanksgiving, and the media was looking for content. As strongly as I spoke, I remember with a smile how the good senator whispered in my ear, "Go easy! You have to deal with Immigration in the coming years."

As with so much in our practice, I can look back to my father's example. Our practice took off thanks to Dad's masterful handling of the media during the Lennon case, where his efforts drew the world's attention. I remember, as a kid during this time, that our "media center" consisted of three televisions mounted on a kitchen table, each turned to a different network newscast. I would lug a huge reel-to-reel tape recorder (all we had at our disposal) from TV to TV, trying to record Dad's voice as he discussed the famous Beatle's case. As the years have gone by, I've become much more sophisticated with the media, and I expect that using both public and private media will be a much more natural thing for my children. Professionally I can categorically state that all my research and well-reasoned arguments are not enough in today's landscape. Amplifying my voice through the media has often been the only way for me to protect the interests of my clients when their applications and pleas were falling on deaf ears within the halls of government.

On a number of occasions, simply keeping my clients in the news kept them alive. I developed a relationship for decades with some of the best court house and beat reporters from Reuters, UPI, and major networks—people who would seek my opinion on matters that our office was consulted on or other matters of national security when they felt my opinion would be worth getting. Going "on the record" and developing an instinct about how to answer a reporter's questions varied from case to case, but the consequences didn't. The treatment we received in an article often influenced the outcome for the client.

I would often be asked to speak as an expert on talk shows, and for years my opinion would then be cited in other cases, and I would find myself being retained by clients on the basis of an old film clip. On many occasions, trying to realize the objectives of a client would mean having to prep myself regarding the handling of a high-profile matter on the fly if I wanted to be available for radio, television, and print media in real time.

In one month, I had two cases involving religion in which the clients had completely different reactions to bringing their cases forward. One individual, facing removal from the United States, followed the instruction of his rabbi, who would not allow him to go public. The other, a mother, sought sanctuary in a church whose public handling of the case was pivotal in developing sympathy. The rabbi may have meant well, but my client was ultimately removed and deported to Europe whereas the church still protects the woman.

Giving a reporter access to a client directly has serious consequences, requiring almost a matchmaker's skill to pair the story and the way it will be told with the appropriate outlet. It's also a matter of calibration: a small, intimate interview; an exclusive; or something much bigger? We've filled our offices on many occasions, multiple rooms crowded with reporters while I brought a client door to door, encouraging open questions.

The Dark Side

The great showman P. T. Barnum is quoted as saying, "There's no such thing as bad publicity." I've also heard the sentiment rendered as "Speak of me well, speak of me ill—but speak of me." My own experience leads me to disagree with these ideas. There can be danger in going public. Throughout my career in politics, as well as my prominence in the immigration field, I took positions that exposed me to significant threats over the years. I don't take the situation lightly—I first received a permit to carry a handgun from the states of New York and New Jersey in the late 1990s. The successful maintenance and compliance to retain these permits, over the last decades, is attributed to my respect and understanding of the immense responsibility associated with its granting and the imminent threats posed in the practice of my profession. The high-profile nature of my work has only become more extensive with the success of our practice and the related media coverage.

As a public figure, former federal prosecutor, and law professor, I am continually called upon to participate in events of significant exposure throughout the region. These events encompass both the political and professional arenas, and I have served as a commentator, host, or leader on behalf of the community. Moreover, my role as a former public official has led me to comment and assist a number of communities affected by U.S. foreign policy. My campaign to prevent the Libyan dictator Muammar Gaddafi from setting foot in New Jersey when I was mayor of Englewood, New Jersey, in 2009 was successful. Since then, the unrest in the Arab world, including the death of Gaddafi, has created an influx of clients from these affected nations. Some of these cases required my interaction and association with intelligence agencies, diplomatic defectors, whistle-blowers, individuals in life-threatening situations, and others who are engaged in or are victims of violence.

Although the extraordinary lives of my clients may have captured the attention of the media, that notice has also drawn the animus of audience members. The news coverage concerning my cases often placed me in an adversarial light, commenting on polarizing issues. The fact that I am frequently vocal on legal and political topics (most notably anti-terrorism efforts and federal immigration policy) has generated a number of reactions and threats in response to my comments. After appearing on major network television broadcasts, particularly on CNN and Fox News, I continued to receive furious emails and threatening phone calls. There have been occasions while I was traveling with my family when I have been confronted with outbursts from individuals who disagreed with my televised comments. Hundreds of my television appearances have later appeared on various YouTube channels, and the commentary threads are often laced with anonymous threats and politically incendiary comments.

I regularly host events and fund-raisers in the security and intelligence sphere, with guests including U.S. senators and members of Congress. Despite the heightened security arrangements for these events, my office and staff have encountered unwanted attention from extremists. An example of such an instance occurred at a private fund-raiser held in my residence. A gentleman protesting my event refused to leave my property until he was directed to depart by retired detectives hired as event security.

For years I was contacted by elected representatives of foreign parliaments and ambassadors from the United Nations seeking political asylum in the United States. Special security measures had to be taken for the consultation with these clients. Some of them had already escaped multiple attempts on their lives by radical adherents of opposition parties. Insurgents firing RPG 7 rockets destroyed their homes, sometimes killing members of their security details. I would not take these cases until these attempts were confirmed by U.S. embassies in those regions. In addition to discussing legal strategies for these cases, I would contact a United States government intelligence service, seek counsel from an agent concerning potential cooperation, and arrange with the local police department for special security measures while my client remained in the New York area. I would see that my clients agreed to consult with me exclusively on these issues (using several approved translators so no one individual would have access to all the information discussed) and that I must be present for all future communications with the United States intelligence services.

In numerous conversations with CIA agents, the first item stressed was that matters be handled discreetly. If leaked, my client's case could become a major news item with diplomatic implications, revealing the inability of particular governments/coalition forces to protect members of their own parliament. To this end, we discussed overseas cooperation between my client and the intelligence services, as well as providing a safe harbor for the filing of applications for the clients' wives, children, and others.

In addition to consulting with leaders and advisors to the upper echelon of the Falun Gong (Falun Dafa movement), I filed a political asylum case on behalf of a client who was a thirteen-year-old, devout Falun Gong practitioner. While on an international class trip to the United States and based on her clear fears of imminent persecution, she expressed a strong desire to remain in the United States with her aunt and uncle. Her relatives attempted to remove her from the tour group while in a McDonald's in Highland Falls, New York. This was unsuccessful, despite the assistance of a police officer. Following the incident, chaperons interrogated my client before trying to force her to return to China. Falun Gong adherents in China are subject to persecution, including the loss of their livelihood and even imprisonment. The last-minute intervention of United States customs agents stopped my client's plane on the runway. The incredible drama surrounding this case drew unwanted attention from the Chinese intelligence services. From my own research, I understood this organization was quite active in the New York region. Now, however, I discovered the reality as threats were leveled against my client, much to the concern of her aunt and uncle. The successful conclusion of this matter garnered great attention and future referrals.

I worked on several cases in volatile regions in the world where both my clients' safety and my own well-being were challenged. These were people in deadly peril, and anyone assisting also risked danger: a Sudanese nationalist attempting to escape the genocide in Darfur; a middle-aged Jewish man living in Belgium who was threatened by Muslim extremists; and an Iraqi Kurd, a national hero in Iraq for his efforts against former President Saddam Hussein's regime, who entered the United States in 1991. All matters were delicately yet favorably disposed.

In March 2005 a client was murdered; Dale Stoeffel was killed "execution style" in Iraq. Although the murder was attributed to his participation in the sale and transport of weapons, he was apparently the subject of a separate FBI investigation involving international matters, which remains open. The intelligence agent who informed me of the situation also told me that the circumstances surrounding my client and the FBI investigation did, in fact, relate to work in which I was involved.

For years I consulted with an individual seeking permanent status in the United States in the wake of his father's tragic political assassination in Algeria. My client was always prayerful that he would resolve his father's murder. Correspondence and meetings ensued, in which he shared with me developments from his own investigations, including confrontations with high-profile government ministers and security officials whom he suspected of being responsible.

In later years I would be visited by leaders of a Syrian-Jewish community concerned over a special immigration dilemma. Members of the community had fled Syria for the United States in the mid-1990s but substantively relocated to Israel. Now, however, they wished to join their brethren in Brooklyn. U.S. immigration law and policy would have considered them to have firmly resettled in Israel, and as such they were ineligible for religious asylum on U.S. soil. To make an exception would require a legislative act. Discussions with several members of Congress and the administration ensued. I suggested a remedy they ultimately employed wherein the interested families were sponsored for green cards through a conventional labor certification by multiple U.S. employers rather than seem unappreciative and wear out the hospitality originally intended and accorded.

When I graduated from law school in the early 1990s, I interviewed for a position as a staff attorney at the Office of Special Investigations— the Nazi hunters in Washington—prosecuting war criminals. I was torn between that job and practicing as a federal prosecutor and ended up opting for a position at the U.S. attorney's office in Brooklyn. Years later, though, I had a chance to step onto that road not traveled when I joined the effort to keep Kurt Waldheim out of the United States. Mr. Waldheim ran for president of Austria in 1971, and he was the UN secretary general from 1972 to 1977. Mr. Waldheim's activities as a German military officer in World War II were subsequently brought to light, causing him to be placed on a "lookout list" (part of the National Automated Immigration Lookout System [NAILS]) used to help officials identify individuals who are excluded from entry into the United States. The World Jewish Congress (WJC) contacted me upon learning that Mr. Waldheim and the Austrian government were interested in removing his name from this list. The WJC asked that I help keep him permanently barred from the United States by ensuring Mr. Waldheim remained on the lookout list. To this end, I prepared the necessary memorandums, and the ban continued until Waldheim's death in 2007. I recall receiving threatening calls in connection with this matter. And even despite his death, neo-Nazis were still perturbed enough to express opinions of me in the most hate-filled manner.

Obviously, the world of national security is one of secrets, but here successful media management is even more important. If the wrong information gets out, people may be killed, operations derailed, or delicate diplomatic undertakings scuttled before they can even begin. The fact is, there are several cases that I'm not permitted to record in these pages due to an agreement with the federal government. For some of those matters, I can't even keep files in our offices. Government agents would visit with encryption devices to record and safeguard our documents and applications (such as filing for political asylum). In this way, we protected the secrets of my clients and the operating methods of the intelligence services working with us.

Many investigative matters were referred to me with regard to anti-terrorism. I was retained by one of the highest-ranking officials in Turkey's intelligence organization who was concerned for his welfare and personal security. For years I worked with Steven Emerson, the director of the Investigative Project, a Washington, DC counterterrorism institute and America's largest private data-gathering center on militant Islamic activities. I acted to secure visas for their analysts and consulted on various anti-terrorism matters. One analyst, Lorenzo Vidino, authored a book titled *Al Qaeda in Europe: The New Battle Ground of International Jihad*. I represented the author on a specialty occupation visa petition. Both parties appreciated my commitment to anti-terrorism, which was reflected in the author's acknowledgments in his book. Other noted international bestselling authors interviewed me and profiled my handling of intelligence-related matters such as Michael Bar-Zohar and Nissim Mishal's 2012 profile of Israel's Secret Service in *Mossad* and Ronen Bergman's

2007 expose and coverage of the world's thirty-year clandestine struggle against Iran, detailing its rise as a terrorist power in *The Secret War with Iran*.

Through the years I have appeared on hundreds of programs and have written extensively with regard to many of the cases and experiences that I have enjoyed. I have hosted or moderated a number of panels on anti-terrorism efforts, such as the New Jersey Terrorism Conference, served as the chairman of the American Jewish Congress (AJC) Anti-Terrorism committee, met with multiple European ministers of justice, and participated with the AJC committee on African-Jewish relations. I have also been solicited by foreign governments for input and advice on anti-terrorism matters, including the witness protection service of foreign nations who were placing individuals safely in the United States to avoid death in their home countries.

On many occasions, I had the police warn me of a threat, watch and protect me from afar during delicate meetings, and respond to my home and offices to assist and protect me and my family. On more than one occasion, someone discovered the car that belonged to me and left notes disapproving of my comments on television/radio. There is a delicate balance in the world of media management when you receive menacing communications. The threats I have received have been specific and detailed. I have on every occasion contacted the appropriate authorities, whether federal or intelligence agencies, and have on occasion hired private bodyguards when suggested or needed at public or sensitive events. There is not a day that I am not concerned about my safety and that of my family: a fatwa was publicly issued against me and has never been rescinded (with regard to an Islamic scholar vilified by extremists whom I represented in the 1990s).

I continue to carry a bulletproof vest in my trunk and have worn it on occasion. I continue to maintain all my carry permits in several states—all are current and have been extended without issue. Arousing public opinion through media management can indeed cut through many obstacles, but it is a two-edged sword. In my practice, a wise lawyer prepares every defense—legal and personal—while hoping they don't have to be used.

— 5 —

The Case of the Disenchanted Diplomat

———

Well-founded fear of persecution. (i) An applicant has a well-founded fear of persecution if:

(A) The applicant has a fear of persecution in his or her country of nationality or, if stateless, in his or her country of last habitual residence, on account of race, religion, nationality, membership in a particular social group, or political opinion;

(B) There is a reasonable possibility of suffering such persecution if he or she were to return to that country; and

(C) He or she is unable or unwilling to return to, or avail himself or herself of the protection of, that country because of such fear.

—*U.S. Asylum Law*

———

Classical scholars may know Saudi Arabia as the land of frankincense and myrrh. Religious scholars may know it as the birthplace of

Islam, where Mecca and Medina remain sites for religious pilgrimage. Few know it only became a nation in 1932, thanks to the conquests of Abdulaziz ibn Abdul Rahman ibn Faisal ibn Turki ibn Abdullah ibn Muhammad Al Saud, known to the West as Ibn Saud, who conquered most of the Arabian Peninsula and gave his family name to his new kingdom. Saudi Arabia is also a family business. An absolute monarchy, all the land belongs to the king, and his family members hold all the most important ministries, provincial posts, even diplomatic positions. Ibn Saud died in 1953 but still has more than thirty living sons.

When the kingdom was founded, most of its income came from taxes levied on pilgrims bound for Mecca. In 1938, oil was discovered, and Ibn Saud was receiving $2.5 million per week at the time of his death. As a son of the desert, the king worried that such wealth would corrupt the frugal lives of the royal family and its austere religious beliefs. He was right. By the reign of King Fahd in the 1990s, the nation's $100 billion cash reserves had been reduced to a mere $7 billion. Royal family members received enormous stipends and lived in a manner frowned upon by the puritanical Wahhabi sect of Islam they were supposed to follow. Princes smoked, drank, and gambled at casinos in London and Monte Carlo. They built enormous palaces, invested in real estate all over the world, and bought expensive clothing and fleets of luxury cars.

Supporting that lifestyle has led to corruption. Historically, Saudi Arabia has been among the top customers for U.S. military hardware. To make these enormous sales, defense contractors regularly offer "commissions" (bribes) to influential government figures—who just happen to be Saudi princes. When the Saudi Air Force paid $5.5 billion to buy five Airborne Warning Control Systems (AWACS) aircraft in 1981, the planes themselves cost only $110 million each. Even adding in maintenance and training, $5 billion in overhead seems a bit steep—and an excellent target for some creative accounting.

Oil money has financed Wahhabi mosques and schools in many countries, spreading this intolerant form of Islam. Whether by clandestine government funding or the donations of wealthy Saudi families, untold millions of dollars have found their way to terrorist groups around the world. The Saudi royals made a bargain with their people, guaranteeing a comfortable living standard for all as the price of absolute authority. To ensure their preeminent position, they have used their wealth to breed chaos among the disparate elements within their own country—and by playing both sides in conflicts around the world.

Even with an extended family numbering in the thousands, the House of Saud can't fill all the positions in the government. They rely on a new generation of college-educated technocrats for many functions. That, however, has brought a new problem. As many Saudis study in foreign countries, they become "contaminated" with Western ideals that are at odds with absolute monarchy. But rebels aren't created merely by outside education. Even a product of the "safe," conservative Saudi universities can become disenchanted. My client, Mohammed Abdulla al-Khilewi, is a case in point.

Khilewi was a member of a wealthy Saudi family, and he studied political science at King Saud University and attained a master's degree from the Institute for Diplomatic Studies. Interestingly, approximately a quarter of his diplomatic training involved intelligence and security matters and spy craft, such as small-arms training, covert communications, and methods of hiding weapons and documents. All Saudi diplomats were issued pistols, and thanks to diplomatic immunity, they could carry them anywhere. Khilewi had assignments in Britain, Switzerland, and the United States. He accompanied the Minister of Foreign Affairs, Prince Saud, and even King Fahd as part of diplomatic delegations.

In 1992, Khilewi was named Second Secretary to the Permanent Saudi Arabian Mission to the United Nations. He worked mainly on nuclear disarmament issues, but he also served as chargé d'affaires, conducting diplomatic business, including voting in the General Assembly. He was promoted to become one of the three First Secretaries at the mission in 1993. Throughout his education and career, Khilewi had harbored growing doubts about the regime in his homeland. His own family had seen repression. Three male cousins had been imprisoned for activities in favor of human rights, and a female cousin was one of forty-five women arrested for driving cars at a mass protest against the ban on females operating automobiles in 1990.

Khilewi's top security clearance brought to his notice numerous terrorist activities undertaken by the Saudi government. Some were directed against groups within Saudi Arabia to help maintain the regime. But there were also international efforts to increase discord between Jews and Muslims, including planned actions against Jewish organizations in the United States. He also found proof of corrupt financial dealings within the government. Determined to prove any charges he brought, Khilewi began compiling a private collection of confidential documents by taking them to the copying center across the street from his office. In time, he assembled some 14,000 pages of secrets, including:

- Financial support for extremist organizations in Egypt, Syria, Pakistan, the Philippines, and Lebanon, not to mention Palestine
- Billions of dollars to aid Saddam Hussein's military during the Iran-Iraq war of 1980–1988
- Military aid to Pakistan, in addition to bankrolling the Pakistani research that resulted in an atomic bomb
- Intelligence and surveillance against American Jewish groups
- Financial irregularities within the Saudi UN Mission, where a check for $9.7 million, issued by the Saudi government to cover UN dues, was used to buy certificates of deposit in New York banks, with the interest diverted to members of the diplomatic staff

On May 17, 1994, Khilewi became convinced that the political situation had reached crisis proportions. Saudi Arabia was preparing for a war with neighboring Yemen to distract the population from the regime's failures. Khilewi prepared a letter for the Grand Mufti, the leading religious figure in the country; Crown Prince Abdullah; other members of the royal family; and members of the Consultative Assembly, the Saudi parliament. In doing so, he apparently followed a tradition (legal and perhaps religious) of using open letters to government figures to publicize a request or belief. Khilewi's letter decried King Fahd as a despot, implicating him in the assassination of his predecessor, King Faisal, and condemning corrupt and divisive activities of the Fahd regime. This was a bold step—even the most serious critics of the government stopped short of denouncing the king.

The response was quick: an offer by the Saudi Ambassador, Prince Bandar, for Khilewi to use his private jet to come to Washington and discuss the matter. Once aboard the private plane, Khilewi knew he could just as easily be taken to Saudi Arabia where torture or even death might await him. His homeland has a number of dire punishments under religious Sharia law—including execution by beheading. Within hours, a Saudi intelligence officer personally threatened him (which Khilewi captured on a voice recorder as he surrendered his pistol). He also received phone calls from his father and his brother back home in Saudi Arabia, reporting that they'd been contacted by the foreign minister, Prince Saud. The tone from various diplomatic staff members quickly progressed from sweet talk to bribery, usual government responses to dissident open letters. But then they became threatening. A so-called diplomat, whom Khilewi always believed to be an agent of the Saudi security service, was blunt: "Go back to Saudi Arabia, or you, your family in Saudi Arabia, your wife and kids will be killed."

Faced with such an unexpectedly bloodthirsty reaction, Khilewi went into hiding. That's where I entered the picture. I had only recently joined my father's law practice, having previously served in the U.S. attorney's office. A former law student of my father's referred Khilewi to us, and my recent government service sealed the deal. Khilewi needed a direct conduit to U.S. law enforcement and hoped my contacts could do that job. For me, this would be an education in immigration law that no law professor had ever touched upon.

Being a political dissident is very dangerous in Saudi Arabia, where political parties are illegal. The government often buys silence— Khilewi was offered millions in hush money. Or the all-powerful royals may just ignore dissidents, attempt blackmail, or engage in a smear campaign. Khilewi was accused of working for Iran, the Israeli Mossad, being a lazy diplomat, and being an agent of the FBI. It seemed, however, that since Khilewi had thousands of pages of secret documents to back up his accusations, a determined faction wanted to take stronger measures— kidnapping or outright assassination.

Accusations that Khilewi worked for the FBI were especially ironic. The bureau did not cover itself in glory with this case. I contacted my former boss at the U.S. attorney's office to arrange a meeting with the FBI. My father and I went to the Hotel Elysee near our midtown offices to meet agents and presented several documents from Khilewi's information trove, describing Saudi intelligence operations on U.S. soil, including assassination plans against Western diplomats. We also shared documents about conspiracies for nuclear proliferation—Saudi government-sponsored funding for an Islamic bomb—which didn't exactly fit the conventional view of Saudi Arabia as a loyal U.S. ally.

You would think the pages were radioactive, the way these counter-intelligence agents acted. They just let the papers sit on the conference table and went outside to call their superiors. These were the days when cell phones were the size of bricks, and I figured the FBI guys had to be racking up quite a bill as they worked their way higher and higher up the chain of command, only to get conflicting orders. What really shocked me, though, was that in the end they told me, "Shots are being called at a high level," and they were told to leave this hard evidence on the table. Apparently, Washington decided it was better to ignore what Khilewi had risked his life to collect and avoid any diplomatic embarrassments with a country that was supplying the United States with a large amount of petroleum, buying a considerable amount of U.S. weapons, and suppos-edly helping to maintain stability in the Middle East. Who cared that he had documentary proof that the Saudis were doing just the opposite? It seemed our government as well as the Saudis just wanted Khilewi and his unwelcome information to go away.

Saudi Arabia has spent millions of dollars on lawyers, public rela-tions firms, and lobbyists to extend its influence on the U.S. government, which includes some of these companies making donations to political action committees. Whenever our story got into the media, the Saudis would buy up whole sections of newspapers such as the *Washington Post* to counter the front page coverage of Khilewi's defection.

Officials in the State Department and other agencies tasked with keeping tabs on the Saudis can look forward to well-paying positions as consultants and executives at Saudi entities after retiring from their government jobs—provided they don't rock the boat. Prince Bandar all but boasted of the policy: "If the reputation . . . builds that the Saudis take care of friends when they leave office, you'd be surprised how much better friends you have who are just coming into office." Even presidents can expect lucrative, Saudi-financed speaking engagements after their terms in office.

It seemed we couldn't expect any help or protection from the FBI. But luckily we were approached by veteran Manhattan District Attorney Robert M. Morgenthau, whom we met with frequently, developing a close personal regard for one another. Morgenthau had been trying to get a handle on criminal activity among the UN diplomatic corps, including money laundering, and hoped Khilewi could help. His office offered practical assistance in the form of a protective detail of NYPD detectives from the DA's squad. When Detective Fred Ghussein started talking to us about security measures, I began to wonder if I hadn't wandered into the pages of a spy novel. He suggested that my client wear a bulletproof vest—and that I should get one for myself for the times when I met with him. Ghussein also trained me to determine whether I was under surveillance, and he encoded certain communications with me in a pager so we did not have to get to a land line telephone. These were the days before cell phones were popular, and in fact I made the transition from a beeper to a personal phone during this case. I felt I didn't have much choice if I wanted to protect myself and my family.

My law firm became a target as well. Our alarm system recorded a break-in at our offices on a Saturday evening. With gun drawn, Ghussein accompanied me to investigate. We found nothing, but the experience led me to engage a security consulting firm who spotted a surveillance camera in the building across the street. They advised us to discuss any delicate topics only in interior rooms and to switch these meetings around to different locations. Using a device to sweep the office for bugs became a regular practice too. Even so, it was obvious that the Saudis had an eye on us. As the case began, my mother had been diagnosed with cancer, a situation we were keeping within the family. Yet when we spoke to the Saudi ambassador, Prince Bandar, he wished for her "speedy recovery." Well wishes conveying a threat—I found that very disturbing.

Prince Bandar was always very cordial in our communications, but he didn't hesitate to refer to us as "Jew lawyers" in private conversation with Khilewi. Needless to say, we didn't put much faith in whatever the prince told us. But it disheartened us, to say the least, to find people we considered friends and allies betraying our trust. Human Rights Watch, an international organization dedicated to publicizing governments' oppression of their citizens, reported extensively on rights organizations arising in Saudi Arabia, and dissidents like Khilewi provided the group with sensitive information . . . only to discover that the officer on the HRW Saudi desk was actually working for the government and turning these secrets over to the Saudi security service.

As if to underscore the amount of influence the Saudis could wield, Prince Bandar stepped in when we seemed to be getting nowhere with our efforts to secure residence and safety for Khilewi. "Mr. Wildes, if your client wants a green card, I can arrange it for him," Bandar said, suggesting we come to his ranch in Virginia to talk it over. Under diplomatic protocol that would be stepping onto Saudi soil, so we declined the invitation. At the same time the ambassador offered this olive branch—a green card if the situation could be handled quietly (i.e., no more embarrassing revelations)—Bandar's uncle Prince Salman, the governor of Riyadh, played bad cop. A delegation of Khilewi's family members arrived in this country, and I arranged for them to meet with Khilewi in Central Park with security from a private investigator. They brought a harsh message from the prince: "Tell your relative we can get him in the United States, we can get him even if he goes to the moon."

The lawyer in me had to wonder. Was this part of a concerted strategy? Or was it an example of royal factions in the government jostling with one another to deal with a defector? One thing was sure; these weren't empty threats. The FBI repeatedly beeped my pager with "911" urgent requests. When I called them, they warned that Saudi intelligence had sent a "team wanting to whisk your client out of here"—credible information that my client was in danger and I might be in harm's way if I were with him. When I asked what could be done to protect a man defecting with important intelligence, they explained that their obligation was to me as a U.S. citizen—and that they'd "fulfilled their responsibility" by advising me of the threat.

This was a period when a number of diplomats had suffered mysterious, fatal "accidents." I faced the question of how to keep my client alive when a government with various rogue players on its payroll wants him otherwise? My answer was to keep him in a glare of publicity. A front-page headline on the *New York Post* screaming, "Kidnap Team Stalks Ex-UN Envoy—Saudi Diplomat Is Terror Target" was probably more effective than a troop of bodyguards. As the only person communicating on his behalf, I waged an aggressive media campaign to keep Khilewi alive, shuttling between different rooms in the office to talk with camera crews from different networks and with print journalists. I felt I pulled off a real coup working with Barbara Walters and the staff of ABC's famed *20/20* news magazine, broadcasting multiple exposés and updates about the case.

We carefully maintained a steady but slow stream of disclosures from Khilewi's information archive—one scoop after another to keep the basic defection story prominent. Journalist Marie Colvin took a report about getting Chinese assistance for Saudi nuclear bomb development and turned it into a front-page story for Britain's *Sunday Times*. A brilliant Middle East expert and front-line journalist reporting on conflicts around the world, she was killed by Syrian artillery in the brutal civil war in that country.

I found it a surreal experience to spend months dealing with regular clients while running a media circus and arranging and attending meetings with Khilewi and the FBI at various times and interesting locales. On a more public stage, Congressman Tom Lantos, cofounder of the Human Rights Caucus (and later chairman of the House Foreign Relations Committee) took a great interest in Khilewi's case. Lantos had a valid historical reason for his human rights concerns—he was a Holocaust survivor. Our visit to Washington was memorable. Not only was it the first time I'd ever worn a bulletproof vest professionally, but I enjoyed a shared ride with a Capitol Police officer armed with automatic weapons. Khilewi and I participated in a closed hearing with no press. Afterward we staged an impromptu press conference on the steps of the Capitol that was reported in the *Washington Post* (the Style section—maybe they thought we were modeling the latest in Kevlar fashion).

At this event I met Steve Stylianoudis, a gentleman of inestimable worth on this case and others. Stylianoudis had an interesting resume, to say the least: besides being an arms dealer, he was also active in public relations—even working for the Saudis. Given his experience and insight, his counsel was invaluable on many delicate Middle Eastern matters.

Throughout the case, the Saudi government tried to downplay the situation, to move Khilewi from the front page to the back pages. Their official response was that Khilewi was merely a disgruntled employee, afraid of being transferred to a posting in an unpleasant African country. He'd claimed asylum to continue enjoying the good life in the United States. In truth, Khilewi had a completely justified fear of persecution if he returned to his homeland. He was officially granted asylum a little more than two months after his application. I counted it a victory when we succeeded in obtaining permanent residency for this brave man. Before joining my father's private practice, I had been a special assistant U.S. attorney, often prosecuting and sometimes fighting to deport undesirable aliens. Frankly, when I first joined my father, I was concerned about being tasked with protecting rogue individuals. In defending Khilewi, I felt I was doing battle for "the good guys."

We asked for special consideration from the INS (predecessor of the USCIS) that they officiate the final resolution of Khilewi's case in our office for security reasons. This was the first time we made such a request, but as subsequent cases will show, it was not the last. When he won his legal residency, Khilewi promised to "fight for the right to live under a democratic system" in his country. He still dreams of a country whose vast wealth is shared fairly, where men and women, the Shia and Christian minorities, and the numerous tribal groups enjoy freedom and safety.

On October 4, 1995, I was in synagogue for Yom Kippur when my pager beeped. I discovered several emergency calls had been made to my office from the FBI, who'd receive information that Khilewi had been murdered in a hotel. I immediately started calling around our circle of friends and associates, and after some anxious time found that Khilewi was fine. He confirmed that the rumor was being circulated by the Saudis—why, he could not say. At the time he was undertaking no dangerous activities, just writing a book. Maybe this was their way of expressing an opinion about that. An interesting side note—later that day, I received a message from the Saudi desk officer for Human Rights Watch. Apparently, a mutual friend of his and Khilewi's had "actually been killed." This was the same human rights activist privy to information of all sorts from dissidents who turned out to be a Saudi double agent. All in all, quite a holy day!

Khilewi has faced more death threats, the most recent in 1998. When terrorists exploded a bomb alongside the USS *Cole* in 2000, killing seventeen sailors, the Office of Naval Intelligence consulted Khilewi regarding possible Saudi involvement, beginning a relationship that lasted for years. He has advised and offered information to a variety of intelligence services, not to mention working as a consultant for author Tom Clancy. Khilewi spoke out about the Saudi connection in the tragic events of 9/11 on several television public affairs shows, which makes it all the more ironic that he was reported by several of his neighbors as a suspicious character in the subsequent terrorism scare. Representing him has brought other Saudi defectors and people with problems involving the Middle East to my office. I've often consulted with Khilewi and used his services as a translator.

As for Saudi Arabia, King Fahd died in 2005, the kingdom's finances having run into deficit territory. Crown Prince Abdullah, one of the Saudi notables who received Khilewi's letter of protest when he defected, became king. Abdullah instituted some reforms—too few, in the eyes of many—and died in 2015. He was succeeded on the throne by Prince Salman, the same man who had threatened to "get" Khilewi in 1994.

Twenty-five years after his dramatic defection, Khilewi, now a fully vetted United States citizen, enjoys the freedom and hospitality of our nation—tempered with vigilance. "Even though protecting anyone who lives in this country is a job for the FBI," he says, "I take my own precautions."

— 6 —

The Reach of Terrorism

(3) TREATMENT OF FAMILY MEMBERS OF
CERTAIN ALIENS—In the case of a principal alien
issued an immigrant visa number under section 203(c) of
the Immigration and Nationality Act (8 U.S.C. 1153(c))
for fiscal year 2001, if such principal alien died as a direct
result of a specified terrorist activity, the aliens who were,
on September 10, 2001, the spouse and children of such
principal alien shall, until June 30, 2002, if not otherwise
entitled to an immigrant status and the immediate issuance
of a visa under subsection (a), (b), or (c) of section 203 of
such Act, be entitled to the same status, and the same order
of consideration, that would have been provided to such
alien spouse or child under section 203(d) of such Act as if
the principal alien were not deceased and as if the spouse or
child's visa application had been adjudicated by
September 30, 2001.

—Uniting and Strengthening America by Providing
Appropriate Tools Required to Intercept and Obstruct
Terrorism (USA PATRIOT ACT)

Terrorism operates on a simple mathematical formula—kill one, frighten thousands. It's a way for small groups to exercise power exponentially beyond their numbers. For most Americans, September 11, 2001, brought a new understanding of terror as thousands died live on our television sets. Terror stopped being something that happened "over there" and became something that threatened our greatest cities. In a 2016 survey of what Americans fear, terrorism made two of the top ten spots. Forty-one percent of respondents believed the nation would suffer a major terror attack in the near future, the second-highest anxiety. And more than 38 percent feared that they personally would be the target of an attack, scoring fourth-highest on the list.

Terror has become a problem that not only reaches around the globe but into our psyches. In my practice, I've seen how it has affected our government, our culture, and our people.

The Terrorist

In legal parlance, being "called to the bar" means a person is admitted to argue a case in court. It's the difference between being a law student and being a lawyer. The phrase has a clubby, almost boozy feel—there are a lot of jokes about "passing the bar." But there is a physical bar in most courtrooms, separating the spectators from the area where the work of the court is done: the desks for the opposing counsels, the clerk's table, the judge's bench, and if necessary, the jury box. In most courtrooms, it's a notional barrier, a low wooden railing.

But as I stepped into court on June 18, 1997, I passed a bar that was no laughing matter. It was transparent, floor to ceiling, and bulletproof. This was a courtroom for terrorism cases, built on the grim assumption that any proceedings here might become a target for extremists. That's what my client was accused of being—someone complicit in killing nineteen Americans. Although I had spoken with him extensively on the phone, I had physically met Hani al-Sayegh only that morning. Skinny, bearded, with a white shirt and a tentative manner, he seemed more like a student. And, indeed, he had extensively studied the Koran. That had led him to trouble in his native Saudi Arabia.

Most people think of two things when it comes to Saudi Arabia—oil and the Muslim religion—an absolute monarchy that uses its oil wealth to command world attention far beyond its size or population. On a closer look, despite sharing the same language and culture, Saudi Arabians have many divisions among low- and high-status tribes, but especially in religion. That might sound strange, discussing a country that's overwhelmingly Muslim, but 10 to 15 percent of the Saudi population follow the Shia sect of the faith. The schism is more than a thousand years old, and it has divided the Middle East. Egypt, Jordan, and Saudi Arabia are predominantly Sunni; Iran, Iraq, and several other states have a majority of Shias.

It's an irony of history that a country known for using petrodollars to disseminate the intolerant, fundamentalist Wahhabi form of Sunni doctrine gets that wealth from its eastern sections, where the population is 75 percent Shia. Shiite Saudis are second-class citizens, discriminated against for government jobs, especially dealing with national security. Shias are restricted from employment in the petroleum industry. Even in the courts, their testimony has less weight than that of their Sunni neighbors. The situation worsened when the Iranian revolution of 1979 created a militant Shiite nation geographically close to the Saudi oilfields. Political repression got worse, with fatwas (religious rulings by important clerics) denouncing the Shias for falling away from the true faith, and even sanctioning the killing of Shia followers.

The political situation only grew more complicated with the first Persian Gulf War of 1990. Iraq's invasion of Kuwait threatened the precious Saudi oil fields, and King Fahd asked for American help, welcoming U.S. troops. The Saudi king is known as the Custodian of the Two Holy Mosques, or Guardian of the two holy cities of Mecca and Medina, which seems a hollow title if Fahd had to depend on foreign, infidel soldiers to do the job.

The end of the war and the establishment of no-fly zones in Iraq meant U.S. airmen had to be stationed in Saudi Arabia, causing more unrest and offering an American target for Arab extremists. The result was the Khobar Towers bombing in 1996. Nineteen Air Force personnel died in their quarters, and hundreds more were injured. Although not as bad as the 1983 barracks bombing in Beirut, where more than two hundred died, that had happened in a war zone. The Khobar blast took place in a nation supposedly at peace, a secure ally of the United States. It was a complicated operation, involving a tanker truck with some 5,000 pounds of explosives, a scout vehicle, and a getaway car. For all the Saudi assurances of wholehearted cooperation, the FBI investigators who arrived the next day should have gotten their biggest clue when they discovered that their hosts had already bulldozed any forensic evidence out of existence. The Saudis made extensive arrests in search of the perpetrators, but U.S. agents never got to question them. That was why, when a young man possibly involved with the bombing ran afoul of Canadian anti-terror immigration provisions in 1997, the FBI was interested indeed. The young man was Hani al-Sayegh.

I became involved thanks to my friend Mohammed al Khilewi, who phoned me after hearing of the situation from a Saudi dissident. Apparently, I was becoming known in Middle Eastern circles, because when Sayegh actually talked to Khilewi, he knew my name! Khilewi knew that Sayegh needed a good lawyer, and the FBI agreed. This was no case of concern over due process for a terrorist. It was part of a political and counterintelligence calculation—a chance for the United States to get hold of a source with insider information on Middle Eastern terrorism. For the last century, our country has leveraged its technology to win wars. From artillery and air power to orbital surveillance, drones, and information intercepts, tech has been our go-to weapon. That hasn't been an unfailing success. In 1998, India arranged a surprise six-bomb nuclear testing series despite observation from our spy satellites. Human intelligence, from agents and sources on the ground, still remains paramount, as our enemies have shown. When the USSR collapsed, the successors of the KGB were quick to adopt the technology of the CIA and Britain's MI6, but they also maintained large human networks.

Another important wrinkle in the al-Sayegh case was the chance to talk to a Saudi terrorist without having to go through the Saudi government, that had its own political agenda regarding what we might learn. Khilewi stressed the opportunity of learning from Sayegh while we could. "If he gets back to Saudi Arabia," Khilewi warned, "something will happen to him." The question was, "How could we hold onto Sayegh, and what could we do to get information out of him?" FBI agents knew they'd have to negotiate a deal and were very forthcoming when I made inquiries. Maybe it's a sign of how unprepared our government was to navigate these murky waters that several agents ended up facing an investigation from the Office of Professional Responsibility, the FBI's internal affairs department, suspected of soliciting my services for a suspect.

As I spoke with Sayegh, he told me the story of a young man who became involved with a group of disaffected youths in his local mosque who were suppressed by the government, and going on a ten-year odyssey through Shia-related extremist groups, Shirazi, Hezbollah al Hejaz in Saudi Arabia, and the group's offshoot in Kuwait. Mainly, however, his connection was with the Iranian Revolutionary Guard, which paid him stipends for his religious education, as well as political indoctrination and even military training with the Lebanese Hezbollah. Although his spirit was willing, his flesh was not up to the rigorous physical demands. Asthma made his training a fiasco, and he found himself relegated to maintaining archives, essentially engaging in a clipping service for the terrorist cause.

Although he did engage in surveillance and fact-finding missions, Sayegh denied any involvement in the Khobar Towers bombing, neither the planning nor the operation. He claimed to be in the Iranian city of Qom, having returned to his religious studies. However, the prosecution had identified him as the driver of the scouting car in the bombing mission, blinking his vehicle's lights to signal the bomb truck to move into position. Sayegh claimed he first heard of the Khobar attack by way of a phone call from his wife. He chose to leave the Middle East because he was sick of persecution for his religious beliefs and politics, traveling to Syria, Italy, and finally flying to Canada after a brief stopover in Boston. Only when he arrived in Canada did he hear from his brother that the Saudi security service was searching for him because of the bombing.

While staying in Ottawa for several months, Sayegh was under surveillance from Canadian security. He applied for asylum but was arrested as a threat to the nation's security. As I entered the situation, Canada wanted to deport Sayegh. The question was, where should he go? Both the American FBI and Saudi security wanted him. My job would be to make the best deal I could for my client, which meant arranging for cooperation with U.S. law enforcement. Sayegh understood the alternative, telling me, "They will chop my head off if I go back to Saudi Arabia."

By this point, I was further along in my chosen career and more aware of the priorities. Essentially, I'd be sitting down in a poker game with the king of Saudi Arabia and the head of the FBI for the life of Hani Sayegh. I made it clear to my client that I would represent him pro bono so long as he cooperated. To me, Sayegh represented a chance for U.S. law enforcement and security to put faces and personalities to the names in the government's transcripts of phone intercepts. Though Sayegh claimed to have little information, government agents believed he was holding back, perhaps because of his family. His wife and two children were in the hands of the Saudis, who had confiscated their travel papers.

Though much of the information he shared has been placed under seal by the government, I believe I can tell one story. Traditionally, Shias use prayer rocks, holy stones that they tap against their foreheads while praying. The practice is frowned upon by the Wahhabi religious authorities, which bans the importation of these holy stones. That doesn't stop the Shias from smuggling them into Saudi Arabia—or Sayegh's group from adding explosives to shipments of the sacred stones.

Sayegh required an interpreter, and as I interviewed him I took the precaution of switching interpreters every fifteen minutes to restrict the flow of information to any particular person. That turned out to be a good call; we discovered one of the Canadian Arab speakers had been compromised by a foreign intelligence agency. Luckily, I was able to depend on loyal friends Mohammed al Khilewi and Steve Stylianoudis to get information from my client.

Certain parts of the case took on a spy novel hall of mirrors aspect. In addition to U.S. security, I dealt with intelligence services from friendly countries, Saudi dissidents in London and elsewhere, and various experts on the Middle East, as well as international journalists. I was very distrustful of foreign media. They might represent legitimate news operations, or they could be foreign operatives trying to familiarize themselves with my daily routine. I never met with them in my office space for interviews, only using public areas and for only brief amounts of time.

I had moved to Englewood, New Jersey, and I have to credit the local government for its efforts in keeping my family safe. They maintained a constant police presence, routing trucks away from our block. Any cars coming onto the street had to pop their trunks, and the police patrolled the perimeter of our property every few hours. Some neighbors kidded me, saying there should be a large sign with an arrow pointing to my house, but for me it was no joke. I started self-defense training and bought a gun. I had a wife and two children to protect, after all.

I represented Sayegh on the immigration side of the deal, but he also faced criminal charges and had an attorney for them. The Canadians deported Sayegh to the United States, and Attorney General Janet Reno had granted an immigration exception for the sole purpose of trying him in a U.S. court for his part in the bombing. I got the news at a Father's Day kindergarten breakfast with my daughter Raquel, then five years old. She managed to spill milk all over herself when my beeper went off. Later that day, the government sent me the government's motion to seal the plea agreement. Because of that seal, I'm still unable to discuss the deal we made. Suffice it to say my client would plead guilty to an earlier, nonfatal plot, which would put him safely in U.S. custody.

I flew down to Washington, finally meeting Sayegh face to face. Up to this point, all our discussions had been conducted over the telephone. I checked into my hotel and met with a score of reporters, congressional staffers, and interpreters before turning to the business of the afternoon. Later I discovered that the scene at my office was even crazier, with requests coming from respected journalists such as Katharine Weymouth, publisher of the *Washington Post*, and requests for exclusives coming from *60 Minutes* and ABC, plus Canadian and European news organizations.

My meeting with Sayegh was spent going over the upcoming court proceedings, although we discussed some of his hopes for the future. Then I was off to the courthouse, finding about sixty news cameras and a good hundred media types waiting for me. Inside the fortresslike courtroom, we went through the usual preliminaries. Then I went outside to discover the crowd of news people had doubled. I kept my comments brief, mainly saying that the proceedings had been placed under seal. It was a very busy news cycle. The same day, after a four-year manhunt, a joint CIA/FBI task force had captured a young Pakistani who had killed two CIA employees. He had sprayed automatic weapons fire at cars entering the gates of the CIA's Langley, Virginia, headquarters. The two stories dominated front pages of newspapers all over the country.

I received less pleasant news when I returned to Sayegh and found him suffering from a stress-induced asthma attack. When I demanded that he get an inhaler, he was sent to a hospital under an FBI SWAT team escort. His FBI handlers also shared Sayegh's medical file. It seemed that the skin test had come back positive for tuberculosis. They suggested I might want to consult with an infectious disease specialist because I had spent hours in close quarters with Sayegh. In the end, I decided to issue a statement about Sayegh's asthma but not to mention the tuberculosis. That I'd get to worry about on my own time.

When I returned to my hotel, I learned that the *Washington Post* had already filed a legal motion on behalf of ABC, CNN, and a whole alphabet's worth of news organizations to unseal the day's court proceedings. I had a busy night on the phone, with perhaps one light moment. My father was in Florida, speaking at the convention of the AILA. He was quite surprised to find a picture of his son on the front page of the *Orlando Sentinel.*

The next hearing in the case had been set for a week away, and I spent the time in conference with the judge, the U.S. attorney's office, the criminal lawyer assigned to the case, and with Sayegh. He was staying in an FBI safe house, his health having improved. The asthma was under control, and a chest X-ray was negative for tuberculosis. Though Sayegh did not seem to be contagious, I was given medication as a precaution.

The client might have been well, but the case took a very bad turn. Instead of pleading guilty to the charges as he had agreed, Sayegh declared himself innocent. I don't understand this decision. Yes, as subsequent events showed, the government didn't have a strong enough case to convict, so they withdrew the criminal charges. But by beating the rap there, Sayegh destroyed his deal. There was still the immigration case, and Sayegh was an avowed terrorist facing deportation. From the outset, I had stipulated that my help for Sayegh was contingent on him cooperating with the authorities. He hadn't done that, so I withdrew from the case.

Hani al Sayegh was deported from the United States on October 10, 1999, and sent back to Saudi Arabia. Supposedly the Saudis had agreed not to torture him. On his arrival, he was held incommunicado at Al-Ha'ir Prison for ten days before his wife and children were allowed to see him. Saudi Arabia is an extremely closed society, and it's difficult to get information out of the country. Was he tried for his reputed association with the Khobar bombing? Was he, as he feared, beheaded? Was he hanged? There is no solid information about his fate.

In 2001, the Department of Justice issued an indictment for several people suspected of involvement in the Khobar Towers attack. Among them was Hani al-Sayegh. For me, it defies understanding how the government could have someone in detention, let him slip through their fingers, and then go through the empty process of indicting him years after he was probably executed. A federal judge ruled in 2006 that the attack was the work of Hezbollah with the help of Iran providing funds, plans, and maps. However, this was a default judgment—the Iranians were not present in court and never had a chance to challenge the assertions against them.

For many people, the question still remains, "Who was responsible for the Khobar Towers bombing?" Based on his knowledge of his homeland, my friend Mohammed al Khilewi believes the Saudi government was somehow involved, playing both sides, the Americans and the Shias, against each other for political benefit. Steve Stylianoudis, who has developed a rare insight into Middle Eastern politics, looked toward the Saudi royal family. Political intrigue is a fairly bare-knuckled pastime among the royals. Crown Prince Abdullah, who was virulently anti-American at the time, might have had a hand in orchestrating the plot. Blowing up some Americans would embarrass his brother, King Fahd, and by implicating Iran, force a harder line against that country. It would also counter the next prince in line for the throne, Sultan (father of Prince Bandar, the Washington ambassador), who was courting the United States to support his ambitions. After all, the year before, extremists had attacked the Saudi National Guard, which was Abdullah's power base in the country.

My own theory on the situation was that the Saudis tossed Sayegh to U.S. law enforcement essentially as a scapegoat because they had withheld access to the other perpetrators. Faced with these terror accusations, Sayegh had lied about his activities, fearful of being deported to Saudi Arabia. The truth will never be known. I find it interesting, though, that sometime after Sayegh was deported, an FBI agent asked if my client had happened to mention a new name in the news . . . Osama bin Laden.

The Victims of Terror

If the Khobar Tower bombing was a wake-up call, the events of September 11, 2001, were a four-alarm fire. Three jet aircraft where hijacked and used as weapons of mass destruction, destroying the World Trade Towers and damaging the Pentagon. Thanks to a counterattack by passengers, a fourth plane failed to complete its attack, although the hijackers crashed it with complete loss of life for all on board. In all, nearly 3,000 people died that day. Almost six hundred had been born in countries other than the United States and were here under various immigration categories. In nearly a hundred cases, victims' families did not request death certificates. Some of these were probably immigrants as well—undocumented immigrants. Whether visiting executives or dishwashers, the loss of life was equally tragic.

But the suffering didn't end there. The death and destruction also left whole families in immigration limbo. In many households, one family member held the green card that allowed residence, and those crashing jetliners had murdered that person. What happened then? I'll tell you the stories of two families I was able to help.

Paul Gilbey was a British national working in the financial field. He and his wife Deena had been living in the United States for ten years. They had two sons who were born here, but neither of the Gilbeys were U.S. citizens. They had applied for green cards in 1994, but Paul had changed jobs, forcing them to begin the procedure all over again. On September 11, Paul was working for a firm called Eurobrokers as a vice president on the eighty-fourth floor of the South Tower. Eurobrokers was one of the few firms that began evacuating its offices after the North Tower was hit at 8:46 a.m. Gilbey helped coworkers get down the stairs. Then the announcement system came on, reassuring everyone that the building was stable and telling them to return to their offices. Gilbey headed upstairs—right into the impact zone for the second suicide airliner.

Deena Gilbey had been getting her older son off to school when a neighbor told her about the first strike. She spoke to Paul, who told her he was leaving the building. That was the last she heard from him, but she spent the day holding onto hope that he had escaped. As evening came, her hope began to fade. She tells a story about talking the matter over with her younger son, and how he suggested that they talk to the police to make sure they were looking for his dad. The local township police were very kind to the little boy who had probably been orphaned.

Deena was still dealing with this terrible news when another blow hit her, this one courtesy of the INS. The Gilbeys had residency in the United States thanks to a long-term work visa in Paul's name. With Paul's passing, that visa expired. Mason and Max, her sons, were U.S. citizens by virtue of being born here. Deena, however, was not—and was told that she faced deportation. This news outraged the local police chief, who joined Deena in a campaign to enlist the aid of politicians on both sides of the Atlantic, as well as talking to American and British media outlets. The sad fact is that the catastrophe left hundreds of spouses and children in the same situation. The government tried to do something for them in the PATRIOT ACT, passed forty-five days after September 11. Most of the bill's language dealt with strengthening national security, but provisions were added to help spouses and children of victims. They were allowed to remain in the United States until September 10, 2002, or until the visa they had depended on expired, whichever came first. Dependents were also allowed to receive green cards—if an application had been made before the September 11 attacks.

That second caveat created a stumbling block for many families. In Deena's case, she was told that although the family had applied for residency in 1994 and had started over when Paul changed jobs, the "paperwork had not reached a certain level of the process," and the application was denied. A lot of people were incensed over this development. My favorite reaction was by the local police chief, who threatened to stand guard with a rifle on the Gilbeys' front porch to keep the INS at bay.

Others took a more nuanced approach. After introducing a bill to extend citizenship to the spouses and children of 9/11 victims in general, New Jersey Senator Jon Corzine added a private bill to naturalize Deena Gilbey and her family. This was backed by other New York and New Jersey senators and read in part, "Paul Gilbey was killed in a callous and cowardly attack on America. In the aftermath of this tragic event, we have a responsibility to help ensure that stability returns to the lives of the children he left behind." Unfortunately, the bill never got to the Senate floor. Many private bills die, usually because the lawmakers don't feel there's sufficient hardship to help an individual. Or perhaps, as Deena heard from an INS agent, there is fear it would set a dangerous precedent. Frankly, I found that response lacking in both sensitivity and heart. But perhaps it is only too indicative of the kind of bureaucratic inertia that had the INS deliver a student visa, six months after 9/11, to the Florida flight school where Mohammed Atta trained for his part in flying a hijacked plane into the Trade Center.

Thanks to the help of the *New York Times*, the *New York Post*, the *Daily News*, and British publications such as the *Daily Mail*, the *Daily Telegraph*, and the *Guardian*, we took the case to the court of public opinion. Though the INS denied it, publicity seemed to have an effect. Grounds for reevaluating the case were found, and Deena faced an hour-long, videotaped interview with immigration officials. The ordeal might have been prolonged until I reminded them that Deena had already undergone vetting by the CIA in relation to the private naturalization bill.

On July 22, 2002, after ten months of stress and struggle, Deena received a green card, allowing her to work and live in this country. For the Gilbey family, however, there is something far more important. "Paul's body has not been found and is unlikely to be," Deena has said. "His grave site will always be the World Trade Center. My children and I are experiencing a genuine longing to reach out and be close to Paul, even if the only way to do that is by visiting his grave site. I simply cannot imagine not living in the country where my husband and father of my children is buried."

The Gilbey case illustrated how terrorism and bureaucratic inflexibility threatened even a rising young banker's family. The story of the Ryjov family featured more of the ups and downs of an immigrant's life.

Vasily Ryjov was an engineer on Soviet vessels, which often took him to ports in the United States. Even though he was disaffected by the Soviet system, he feared to jump ship because of the repercussions for his family back home. When his wife Tatiana was sent to the United States as a translator, she took their two-year-old son and never came back. Pressured by the KGB, Vasily divorced Tatiana and still lost his job.

The couple was determined to reunite, and in 1991 Tatiana successfully petitioned for a tourist visa to bring Vasily to the states. They were remarried, and another son was born in 1993. Vasily tried to apply for asylum but was rejected. He wound up paying $4,000 to someone he thought was an immigration lawyer to get a work permit. This process involved signing several papers, even though Vasily didn't read English. In the end, he received a work permit and continued working in construction even after the permit expired. The person who was supposed to help him disappeared with the money, but Vasily thought things were okay. As he explains, "I was paying taxes, buying a house, raising a family. If I knew I did something wrong, I would be staying low, wouldn't I?"

It wasn't an easy life, but as Vasily says, "When you live in former USSR and you have almost no rights, you kind of hope for better future for your children. You can sacrifice a lot." Tatiana went into the computer field and applied for a green card in 1996. In 2000, they bought a house in Westchester, New York. Then, in 2001, they received wonderful news—Tatiana had won a spot in the annual green card lottery! Officially known as the Diversity Visa program, this lottery gives people from countries with a low rate of immigration a chance to get a visa for the United States, but at very high odds—50,000 visas out of eleven million entrants. That Tatiana managed to win was a piece of incredible luck.

But only four months later, the family's luck turned. Tatiana was working on the ninety-first floor of the South Tower during the terrorist attack. At least in her case there were some remains that were identified by DNA analysis. In a news interview, Vasily cupped his hands to show the pitiful size of the sample. But when he tried to recover those remains, he received another shock. The INS was denying his residency application. According to their records, among those unintelligible documents he'd signed eight years previously were some bogus marriage documents. To the immigration authorities, this constituted fraud—and a valid reason to reject Vasily's application.

Vasily was crushed. "I don't have a wife. I don't have a green card. And I'm going to be deported." That was the situation we faced as I took the case. My first job was to prove that fraud had been attempted but that Vasily had been the victim rather than the perpetrator—and we did so. We also sought to mobilize public opinion in Vasily's favor through media appearances, and we reached out to political figures for help.

New York Senator Charles Schumer quickly came to our support, saying, "With all they've been through, deporting a family who had suffered such a loss in the World Trade Center attacks would be unconscionable. Part of their lives was shattered on September eleventh. It would be a shame to shatter their dream of remaining in America." With the senator taking an interest, we were able to persuade immigration officials to revisit the case, especially in light of the PATRIOT ACT's sections on providing green cards for surviving spouses and children.

The case also attracted considerable public sympathy. A female Wall Street executive, someone who didn't even know Vasily, called us, offering to marry him to improve his status. We don't do that kind of thing in our practice, but it shows how the story had touched people's hearts. It took longer to resolve the Ryjov case favorably. The older, foreign-born son, Alex, got a green card, and in the end, so did Vasily. Personally, I found it reflected very poorly once again on our business-as-usual bureaucracy that so much time went by. These are people who suffered unimaginable loss on our soil. The least we could say is "You're one of us now." Those children shouldn't have had to deal with lawyers and bureaucrats. What they needed were psychiatrists and family therapists to help them overcome the pain.

One result of the 9/11 attacks was a roundup of immigrants—documented and otherwise—in the following months. Fear ran high in the immigrant community, so high that people were consulting me at my home in Englewood because they were afraid to be seen entering the offices of an immigration attorney. Even today, fear of terrorism scars the national psyche, pitting two of our greatest rights—life and liberty—against one another. Finding a balance that protects both is a challenge to our very democracy.

The Hero

The year 2001 was not to end without another terror incident on an airliner, this one threatening the lives of 197 people. Air France Flight

63 took off from Paris headed for Miami, full of people traveling for the holiday season. One of them, however, was a terrorist, the heels of his shoes filled with enough plastic explosive to blow the plane out of the sky. In this case, however, the terrorist was foiled, thanks to the efforts of several passengers, including Kwame James, a young professional basketball player. He had been playing on a team in France and was heading home to Trinidad for the Christmas holidays, with a stop in Miami to pick up his girlfriend. Facing a seven-hour flight in a coach seat, he had stayed up the night before in hopes of dozing through an uncomfortable journey.

While the plane was over the Atlantic Ocean, a flight attendant discovered passenger Richard Reid using a match, attempting to light a fuse connected to a shoe in his lap. Reid, a British citizen with loyalty to the terrorist group al Qaeda, was having difficulties detonating the explosives hidden in the shoe, which apparently had been dampened by perspiration from his feet. The six-foot-four, two-hundred-pound Reid floored the flight attendant and fought with another as other passengers became involved in the fray.

At six feet, eight inches, James was the biggest man on the plane. He was awakened from a sound sleep by a flight attendant, stood dumbfounded for a moment and then helped to subdue the terrorist, who was then tied in his seat with plastic handcuffs, belts, and headphone cords. As fighter planes escorted the airliner, which diverted to Boston's Logan Airport, James stood guard over Reid for nearly four hours, fearing there might be another bomb on the plane or additional terrorists.

The plane landed at its alternate destination and James was hailed as a hero. After the horror of 9/11, the American public went wild for the story of a group of passengers overpowering a terrorist on an airplane— it was a holiday present for a battered nation. James had attended high school in Indiana and played on the University of Evansville basketball team, but he was not a U.S. citizen. He was born in Canada and raised in Trinidad and Tobago and had a worldwide career. In addition to France, he had played ball in Argentina, Korea, and Switzerland. After a barrage of calls from media outlets, James was contacted by government investigators and prosecutors, who promised to arrange a visa for him to stay in this country as a witness against Reid. However, James's testimony wasn't needed. Reid subsequently pleaded guilty and received a life sentence for his abortive attack.

The would-be shoe bomber would reside in the United States for the rest of his life—albeit in a super-max prison—but the man who had helped subdue the villain in this incident faced immigration problems. After returning to France, James came to the United States on a tourist visa hoping to get into an NBA team's development program, but he was cut from a position on the Gary Steelheads, a minor-league basketball team. Government officials admitted that James's case was "compelling," but immigration rules do not include visas for training athletes, nor is the government allowed to fast-track a visa application—even if the applicant is a hero. I came into the case in 2003, criticizing the decision: "Is this the message you want to send to someone who looked down the face of terrorism? It was a national disgrace." On live television, I offered to take James's case on a pro bono basis.

Meeting my new client was quite an experience. By no means do I consider myself a small guy. But I barely came up to the shoulder of this young man. We made several media appearances together, and I personally brought James's plight to the attention of then-Senator Hillary Clinton and Congressman Joseph Crowley. "What he did, instinctively jumping up and subduing Richard Reid, this is what citizenship is about," I argued. "He instinctively did the right thing. He is a hero and a model citizen." I successfully arranged for an advance parole for James, which allowed him to come and go from this country, and with the help of the Brooklyn Kings, a team in the United States Basketball League, I applied for a P-1 working visa.

James eventually married a U.S. citizen. I had the privilege of helping him apply for his green card and years later, in 2010, for his own U.S. citizenship. Thus, in the end, the Department of Homeland Security relented, and James received the right of residency. "This sends a strong message to the victims of terrorism and the people who help," I commented at the time. "We will not leave you behind." Indeed, James has moved forward. Although he did not fulfill his NBA dreams, he did bring his basketball career to a successful conclusion playing on another French team. He tried his hand as a motivational speaker and as a professional trainer and also put his college degree in international business to work, taking a position in the pharmaceutical business. Still married to the young woman he had boarded Flight 63 to meet, he now lives in Georgia and works in information systems.

I never met a man less willing to play the hero card—James always felt there were many others on the plane who deserved recognition for subduing Reid. He has often expressed the wish that his fame had never happened. But he is glad for his opportunities as an American. "I became a citizen of one of the best countries in the world," he said after his naturalization. There are at least 197 reasons the United States should be glad to have him.

— 7 —

The SEAL and the Villager

The term "refugee" means: any person who is outside
any country of such person's nationality or, in the case
of a person having no nationality, is outside any country
in which such person last habitually resided, and who is
unable or unwilling to return to, and is unable or unwilling
to avail himself or herself of the protection of, that country
because of persecution or a well-founded fear of persecution
on account of race, religion, nationality, membership in a
particular social group, or political opinion.

—*Immigration and Naturalization Act*

*As the longest U.S. conflict enters its sixteenth year, the U.S. gov-*ernment has recently announced it will dispatch several thousand additional troops to the war in Afghanistan. From the Afghan side, it's even worse. Since the Soviet invasion of 1979, the Mujahideen insurgency, the Taliban's fight for dominance, various civil wars, the overthrow of the Taliban, and finally, U.S. and NATO involvement, there's been some sort of war going on in Afghanistan for almost the last forty years. And, just in the years U.S. troops have been in the country, an estimated 170,000 civilians have died. This is the story of one Navy SEAL and one Afghan civilian, and our struggle to make sure the Afghan didn't end up as one of those statistics.

The year was 2005. After being dislodged from power, Taliban supporters had taken refuge in remote regions of Afghanistan, fighting a guerrilla war. Kunar province was perfect for the insurgents; it is a rugged section of the Hindu Kush mountains bordering on Pakistan's wild tribal region, which provided both sanctuary and supplies.

As a part of Operation Red Wings, a four-man Navy SEAL team was sent on a recon mission, scouting a group of buildings used by guerrilla leader Ahmad Shah as safe houses. The SEALs encountered a group of local sheepherders and faced a fateful decision—to eliminate these civilians or let them go. Shortly after releasing the herders, the SEALS came under enemy fire. Their attempts to call for help resulted only in reporting that they were under attack without giving their location. This delayed the implementation of a Quick Reaction Force, which took enemy fire when it arrived. A rocket-propelled grenade took out the rotor of one of the rescue helicopters, causing it to crash. The eight-man crew and the eight SEALs aboard were killed. The ambush also took the lives of three of the four members of the original recon team. Only one American, Marcus Luttrell, survived. Severely wounded and stranded in enemy territory, the SEAL's predicament was serious indeed, and his survival depended on the help of an Afghan villager.

Mohammad Gulab found Luttrell, took him to his village, and gave him shelter. He did this in accordance with the *Pashtunwali*, the traditional way of the Pashtun people. For seventeen centuries, this code has prized physical courage (*tora*), revenge (*badal*), hospitality (*melmestia*), and asylum for the hunted (*nanawatai*). For several tense days, the Taliban repeatedly demanded the American. When bribes failed, they turned to threats against the village, but Gulab stood firm. In the meantime, another villager smuggled a note to U.S. forces, and they swooped in, returning Luttrell to safety.

Marcus Luttrell returned to his SEAL comrades, and then to the United States, where his story became a bestselling book, *Lone Survivor*, and then a blockbuster film. Ahmad Shah briefly enjoyed a high reputation for dealing the biggest setback to the Americans since their invasion. The ambush had been videotaped and used as propaganda, and he had captured a lot of weapons and equipment. Subsequent U.S. action, Operation Whalers, burst that bubble, thoroughly defeating the guerrillas and driving a wounded Ahmad Shah into Pakistan. He died there in 2008 in a shootout with government forces.

For Gulab, however, the rescue of Luttrell marked the beginning of a decade of terror. He remained in the war zone, facing considerable hostility for his decision to help the American. His family was forced to flee from their home village, leaving behind their timber and taxi business as well as their farmland. Gulab got a job working at the U.S. base in the provincial capital, Asadabad. But even there, when walking outside the town with his brother-in-law, he came under fire from Taliban snipers. Gulab escaped, but his brother-in-law was struck in the ribs. U.S. servicemen airlifted them to a doctor.

After five years, Gulab managed to get in touch with Luttrell, now a successful author/motivational speaker, and was invited to the United States. But just before he was to set off, Gulab stepped outside his house and a pair of guerrillas on motorcycles fired pistols at him. He leaped for cover, but a ricocheting bullet caught him in the thigh. Gulab had an emotional reunion with Luttrell when he arrived in the United states, and he got to see some of the country. They discussed the idea of getting a green card for Gulab, but the Afghan just wasn't ready to leave his country. He returned home to discover some new reasons to leave. The Taliban hijacked his truck and the load of timber on board. In the United States, Marcus Luttrell organized a fund-raiser for Gulab and the villagers who'd helped him years before. American friends in Afghanistan helped the Gulabs move again, but they had no means of making a living. For a while, the move seemed to bring safety. But one evening as Gulab rode in his nephew's car, he became a target again. Gulab escaped but his nephew was struck in the head and died. That shook Gulab.

In the United States, *Lone Survivor* had gone from a book to the movie screen, and Luttrell wanted Gulab to return to the United States to help with promotion. Gulab was torn. The film would be a recognition of what he and his fellow villagers had done, but it would also stir up the

Taliban even more. In the end, it was the promise that some of the movie money would finance a way to safety, either in Afghanistan or some other country, that swayed Gulab to come. This time he explored the green card option, but it seemed difficult to secure. Advised to seek asylum instead, Gulab hesitated. Whether through faulty translation or misunderstanding, he thought he would never be able to return to his homeland or see his family again.

Relations between Gulab and Luttrell also cooled somewhat. Gulab's recollection of the events of Operation Red Wings differed from the version Luttrell had published in *Lone Survivor*, and the Afghan began to feel that his American friend was not working as hard to help him as he could have. Gulab didn't save Luttrell in hopes of a reward. But now he found himself in financial need, and the situation was about to get worse. The United States was drawing down its troops in Afghanistan, which meant less protection for those who had befriended or helped the Americans. And the publicity around *Lone Survivor* made Gulab particularly notorious.

Gulab might be a hero in the United States, but in Afghanistan he was a marked man. A walk in the woods almost became fatal when the Taliban detonated an improvised explosive device (IED) to get him. Insurgents launched an assault on his home, and Gulab and his wife spent the night firing into the darkness to keep them at bay. Gulab took to sleeping by day with an AK-47 by his side and going into hiding, always in different places, by night. Several attempts were made to detonate explosives near his house. In one case, a blast mildly injured his daughter, and the family was too frightened to go outside until daybreak to take her to the hospital. Perhaps more insidious were the constant threats. The Taliban's shadow governor for the region published a tirade against Gulab. "This letter is from the brave fighters and the mujahideen of the Islamic Emirate," it began. "Your Jewish friends cannot save or protect you. I hope the suicide bombers or the Taliban brothers will fulfill my order. Soon, they will send you to the grave."

Now Gulab regretted leaving the United States, where he could have applied for asylum. The case was referred to me to see what I could do to save this man's life. I suppose that did make me a "Jewish friend" of Mohammad Gulab. Certainly, it brought me to the attention of the Taliban and gave me a taste of what Gulab had been living through. One day as I walked into my office, I received a phone call on my private line. "We know who you are," an Arabic-accent voice told me. "We know you are a Jew, and you should be listening and watching your TV to see what we do to people like you." The mystery caller went on, "As for your client Gulab, we will terminate him and anyone that would help him." It was a shock to receive a threat from people who knew enough about me to reach me directly and not through the office receptionist. I reported the incident to the authorities, but also I redoubled my work.

On the face of it, the job might appear to be easy. As far back as 2008, Democrats and Republicans came together to pass an act offering thousands of visas to Afghans who worked with the U.S. military, either as interpreters or in other jobs, and who now found themselves in danger from terrorists. Unfortunately, the bureaucracy involved in those visa applications can result in literal fatal delays—people were killed before they could leave the country. Undoubtedly, there is a strong need for careful vetting in the name of national security, but the snail's pace of processing—often years—is not merely frustrating, it can be terrifying.

Had Gulab applied for asylum while he was still in the United States, he probably would have been successful. In Afghanistan, he had first to apply for a visa from a U.S. embassy, which itself is essentially in a state of siege. Then layers of bureaucracies had to be penetrated; not just the U.S. Department of Homeland Security and the State Department's Refugee Admissions division, but the international machinery of the UN's Refugee Agency. Even with intense lobbying from U.S. political figures, we received high-flown sentiments but very little action. I decided to take the case public, hoping to get a little more leverage through multiple appearances on international media. In fact, the story of Gulab's odyssey became a cover story on *Newsweek* magazine. Still, the bureaucratic machinery seemed to be at a standstill. Meanwhile extremist assassins were circling in the water. The U.S. embassy sent a recommendation to Washington that bringing Gulab to the United States would serve U.S. interests, but they also warned that they could not guarantee his safety out of Kabul.

We decided on a desperate course to get Gulab out of Afghanistan and into India with his eldest sons. With their primary target gone, perhaps the Taliban would cease their threats. With borrowed money, Gulab boarded a plane for New Delhi. Anxious months followed as Gulab managed to bring the rest of his family to join him. It was a tight squeeze, Gulab and his family were living in a small apartment, barely able to keep a roof over their heads, as they waited—waiting for the U.S. government's security checks to be completed. Nine excruciating months passed, and administratively speaking, Gulab was considered lucky. Some applicants waited five to six *years* before their entry was approved. At last, however, visas arrived, and the Gulabs set off for the United States.

Mohammad Gulab settled in Texas, free at least from the fear of ambush by the Taliban, but he still faces considerable challenges. In his mid-forties, the illiterate mountaineer struggles to learn English and to deal with America's consumer culture. The flatland urban sprawl of Fort Worth is a far cry from the rugged, sparsely populated mountains and valleys he knew. Going from a position of respect in his village, owning his own businesses, he now struggles to find work. His sons, who speak better English, must help to support the family, but all hope to put their resources together and establish some sort of family business.

Gulab no longer sleeps with a Kalashnikov rifle at his side, but his twelve-year ordeal has marked him. He hopes to fade into the background of American life, but he cannot forget that the United States seemed to turn its back on him. If he had hesitated so long ago to help Marcus Luttrell, all that would remain of the American SEAL is a pile of bones beside a waterfall. Understandably, no one wants to go down in history for allowing the next terrorist attacker to get into this country. But when bureaucratic timidity manages to get America's friends killed before they get here, that doesn't serve the nation's interests either.

An iconic shot from my father's defense of John Lennon against deportation— Lennon offering peace to the world from the steps of the federal courthouse.

In all the years since that landmark case, our families have remained close—and Yoko Ono Lennon has remained a favorite client.

Mamadou Soumare, center, who lost four children and his wife in a 2007 fire that killed ten people in the Bronx with me at Federal Plaza. Mr. Soumare was an illegal immigrant from Mali. I received formal permission from immigration officials for my client to re-enter the United States after travelling to West Africa to bury his family. Ozier Muhammad/The New York Times/Redux.

Rather than hide in the face of kidnap and assassination threats, we took Mohammed al-Khilewi's case public—very public—flanked by armed bodyguards and wearing bulletproof vests with a press conference outside the Capitol building.

Meeting Hani al-Sayegh, the accused Khobar Towers
bomber, I looked into the face of terror—and found
a mild-mannered, almost confused client.

Media madness and large bulletproof glass separated me from
the public in Federal court during a 1997 terrorism matter.
Often I would feel safer in crowds and comforted by the
lights of the cameras knowing the world was watching.

When Iftikhar Khan Chaudry defected with information on Pakistan's involvement with nuclear proliferation, a well-orchestrated media campaign branded him a fraud. Yet, years later, the facts turned out to support his story.

Then-Senator Hillary Rodham Clinton joined our effort to help Kwame James when, after thwarting the infamous shoe bomber, James faced immigration problems.

An international child kidnapping case with a positive outcome. We worked with law enforcement agencies to rescue Mary Hamouda's three children and ensure the father who absconded with them got prison time.

Beauty and the lawyer—I handled the immigration concerns for the Miss Universe contestants in 2010.

You've got to bring your best game when you're
dealing with a soccer legend like Pele.

No, that's not me posing with a cardboard cutout. I had the honor and responsibility of clarifying Melania Trump's immigration history during the runup to the 2016 election. Over the years I have also represented the First Lady's parents and sister on immigration matters. Despite the political divide, we developed a close personal relationship.

The two loves of my life—family and public service—both on display for my swearing-in as mayor of Englewood, New Jersey, in 2007.

Sometimes you step into the public spotlight with famous icons . . .

. . . and sometimes you have to face the cameras alone.

The author and
Master Chef
Jean Georges.

Mayor Wildes at Englewood's Memorial Day Parade, 2006.

The author chats with President Bill Clinton.

With Amalija and Viktor Knavs, parents of U.S. First Lady Melania Trump, visiting the Jacob K. Javits Federal Building in New York City.

Attending private reception at the White House with President and Mrs. Trump, December 2017.

The author at a Bar-Ilan University ceremony
with President George H. W. Bush.

In NYPD uniform.

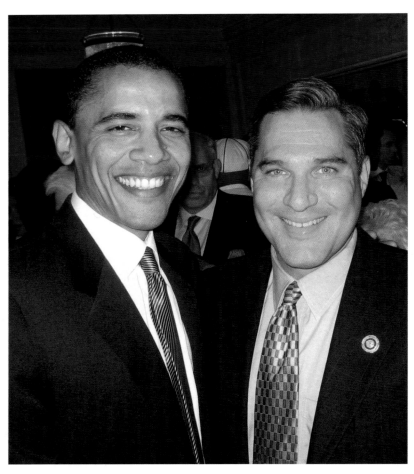

President Obama and Michael Wildes.

With Congressman Tom Lantos discussing the
defection case of Mohammed al-Khilewi.

Being sworn in in 2007 as mayor of Englewood, New Jersey. I am flanked by my wife, Amy, and our four children. Officiants were Rabbi Shmuel Goldin and Pastor Lester W. Taylor, while my father, Leon Wildes, held two Bibles (each used by my grandfathers Max Schoenwalter, who escaped Nazi Germany, and Harry Wildes).

— 8 —

The Nuclear
Whistle-Blower

I, Dr. Iftikhar Khan Chaudhry, permit the U.S.
government to disclose the contents of my asylum
application with the appropriate British authorities and
with Dr. Altaf Hussein in order to establish the veracity of
my claimed identity, former employment, and my claimed
contact with Dr. Hussein during January–May 1998.

It is my understanding that Dr. Hussein has left
Pakistan and has applied for political asylum in the
United Kingdom.

—*Confidentiality Waiver to USCIS*

---

*Recent news is very depressing. North Korea is provocatively run-*ning nuclear bomb tests while complaining that President Trump has declared war on them via Twitter. The U.S. president is threatening to decertify the multilateral treaty with Iran regarding its nuclear program and impose new sanctions on that country for failing to adhere to the spirit of that agreement. In both cases, the root of the problem goes back more than forty years and can be traced to a single man, a man whose name few Americans have ever heard.

In April 1974, the world had five official nuclear powers: the United States, the USSR, Britain, France, and China. That turned out to be an April Fool's paradise, because a month later the club gained a new member when India detonated its first nuclear device. That was a big day for India, but a dark moment for Pakistan, India's long-time antagonist in South Asia. President Ali Bhutto announced that Pakistanis would "eat grass, if necessary," to develop a nuclear deterrent.

In the years since 1947, when the British holdings on the Indian subcontinent were divided into Hindu and Muslim nations, Pakistan and India have engaged in three major conflicts: in 1947 and 1965 over the state of Kashmir, and in 1971 when Indian forces intervened in a Pakistani civil war and East Pakistan became the independent Bangladesh, costing the Pakistani government nearly half of its former population. In the face of such defeats and humiliations, Pakistan began a nuclear project.

This clandestine effort continued for more than two decades and brought a Pakistani scientist, Dr. Abdul Qadeer Khan, to prominence as the father of the Islamic bomb. Khan was ready to use fair means or foul to accomplish his goal. An early coup involved stealing the plans for a centrifuge, a device necessary to concentrate enriched uranium for nuclear reactors—or bombs. The 1980s saw several Pakistani efforts to create subcritical nuclear devices. But the *djinni* really came out of the bottle in 1998, after the Indian government went ahead with a set of five nuclear tests in quick succession. The Pakistanis responded with five nuclear explosions of their own, and a sixth for good measure, officially announcing the existence of an "Islamic bomb."

This was a situation of grave concern for the international community, whose efforts were to limit, not encourage, nuclear proliferation. The sad fact of the matter was that Pakistan did not have the most stable government. Ali Bhutto had taken office after the failure of a military government. He was overthrown by a military coup and subsequently executed. His daughter, Benazir Bhutto, became prime minister after the death of a military dictator but lost the next election, which was rigged by the country's intelligence service. She went into exile, and another military coup took place. When elections were allowed again, Bhutto returned to become prime minister, only to be assassinated by a suicide bomber. In its seventy year history, Pakistan has had three constitutions, which often have been suspended by the military. In fact, the military has governed for a good half of the country's history.

Despite these many problems, Washington has cut Pakistan a lot of slack. Pakistan has been one of the few developing countries that has supported U.S. policies. During the Cold War, it was a bulwark against the expansion of Soviet influence in South Asia. After the Soviet invasion of Afghanistan, Pakistan was an important conduit for aid to the mujaheddin freedom fighters. When the mujaheddin morphed into the Taliban and U.S. troops went to fight in Afghanistan, Pakistan offered an important supply line for the war against terror. As an ally, however, Pakistan definitely had shortcomings. After al Qaeda was driven out of Afghanistan, Osama bin Laden hid out very comfortably in a compound in Pakistan.

After the 1998 nuclear tests, the Clinton administration established sanctions to punish the Pakistani government's actions. With the arrival of a new administration in 2000, however, the sanctions and investigations into Pakistan's nuclear program were halted. Then came 9/11, and the need to placate an important strategic partner in the war on terror eclipsed any lingering interest in checking out any wrongdoing. The highest levels of our government chose to turn a blind eye to Pakistan's nuclear dealings, but that became impossible when a Pakistani defector arrived in the United States in May 1998—a man who claimed to work in Pakistan's nuclear program. In Iftikhar Khan Chaudhry's application for asylum, he revealed secrets about China's role in developing Pakistan's bomb and Iran's payment of billions of dollars for Pakistani nuclear technology. He also raised the specter of a real nuclear nightmare.

A new, more nationalistic administration took over after the Indian elections in March 1998, and it was expected to take a harder line on the Kashmir problem. As Pakistan prepared its own nuclear arsenal, a top-level meeting was held in April among military leaders and members of the Pakistani atomic energy commission. Among the conferees was Chaudhry, a young physicist working for one of the chief researchers. Chaudhry had spent most of his life believing Pakistan needed nuclear weapons as a deterrent, a defensive weapon to maintain a balance of power. However, when representatives of Inter-Service Intelligence discussed the possibility that India would use atomic weapons on the disputed dividing line in Kashmir, he was horrified to hear plans for a first strike being debated that would use Pakistan's new nukes to attack the Indian capital, creating huge civilian casualties.

Along with four other similar-minded colleagues, Chaudhry drafted a letter to his superior, begging restraint and warning that if the proposed attack remained unchanged, he and his cosigners would go public to try and save people from "such a huge atomic collision of two countries." Perhaps some good came from this stand, and the attack did not take place. On a personal level, however, Chaudhry's life blew up. His superior, Dr. Hussein, warned that "you could get killed if you reveal your political beliefs." Pakistan's bomb was important to the whole Islamic world, and his young assistant had put himself in considerable danger. This became increasingly clear in the following days.

Chaudhry was dismissed from his position, along with the others who'd signed the letter of protest, and had his assets frozen. He received a threatening phone call at his home from an agent of Inter-Services Intelligence and immediately went on the run. He had come to fear a nuclear showdown between India and Pakistan months earlier and had arranged for visas to take his family on a visit to Kenya. That plan was short-circuited when government agents kidnapped Chaudhry's wife. He discovered this painful information in a phone conversation with his father's family, when his four-year-old son reported that several men had searched his house, "looking for Papa," and then "they took Mama." He realized he'd have to flee alone. Through friends he was able to get a Canadian visa and was smuggled into the Islamabad airport, where he boarded a plane for Dubai, continuing on to Frankfurt, and then to Montreal. Chaudhry arrived in Canada on May 9, 1998. The Indian nuclear tests began on May 11.

Those tests represented one of the great failures of U.S. intelligence, coming as a complete surprise. The Indian government managed to hide its preparations from U.S. spy satellites by dressing its physicists in army uniforms to camouflage their visits, working at night, and carefully contouring excavations to make them look like wind-created sand dunes.

On May 22, Chaudhry set off on a train to New York City. The first Pakistani nuclear test was detonated on May 28. By June 15, Chaudhry had obtained legal representation, and on June 18 he approached the FBI. We went public with our request for asylum on July 1, giving a press conference in which Chaudhry revealed that he had seen paperwork about funding for nuclear experimentation coming from Saudi Arabia and the United Arab Emirates. During tours of Pakistani nuclear sites, he had seen Chinese visitors in civilian clothes but with military demeanor on site, as well as visiting Iranian scientists apparently eager to learn about Pakistani progress toward a bomb.

The government of Pakistan was quick to dismiss Chaudhry's credentials. The Pakistani UN ambassador claimed that Chaudhry was in fact a low-level nuclear engineer who had worked in Pakistan's atomic program in the 1980s before disappearing. That would have meant that Chaudhry had been handling nukes while he was in high school. Government sources also described the defector as a disgruntled physics graduate student who refused to return home from abroad. The Pakistani foreign minister, Ayub Gohar Khan, described Chaudhry as "an impostor . . . well tutored in the recent past by an intelligence agency." Then a businessman, Gulzar Sheikh, appeared on Pakistani television claiming that he recognized my client as an assistant accountant for a company making ceramic tiles and bathroom fixtures. That company made a statement shortly afterward saying that neither Sheikh nor Chaudhry had worked there.

Chaudhry simply stuck to his story as a variety of tales came out of Pakistan, each one a new attempt to discredit him. At the same time, considerable pressure was aimed at the Chaudhry family, who was told, "your son is leaking state secrets to the enemy." Chaudhry's father lost his job, was arrested, and was coerced into appearing on Pakistani television to help discredit his son. The day after our asylum request went public, Chaudhry's wife was released, but she was raped by government agents before she left their custody.

In New York's close-knit Pakistani community, Chaudhry was a pariah because of his opposition to what the Pakistani on the street considered a great step forward for their nation and for their religion. It was bad enough that crowds chanted for his death in his hometown, but the friend who had sheltered him in his apartment discovered a shocking voice mail message. "We will burn your house. We will kill Dr. Iftikhar Khan," a voice announced in Urdu, the Pakistani language. "We will kill you all."

It's understandable that Chaudhry was under considerable stress when he was interviewed by a pair of visiting Pakistani researchers to establish his bona fides. The idea was to question his knowledge in his native tongue. Whatever the reason, his responses were not impressive during the phone interview. The *Washington Post* and the *New York Times* both ran damaging stories after this. The other four scientists who had signed the warning letter with him could not be found. They had apparently also fled Pakistan, finding refuge in Europe. Based on his own experiences, Chaudhry thought they were probably wise to keep their heads down.

Concern for his safety led Chaudhry to leave New York for Pennsylvania, where he was contacted by a person with Pakistani intelligence to try and arrange a "sit-down" with ISI agents. Chaudhry moved again, this time to Minnesota, where his prospects seemed to grow dimmer and dimmer. The U.S. government, initially interested in what he had to say, felt that they could develop better sources. In his homeland, yet another coup put a military government in place, with martial law. Chaudhry's family warned him that they were under increased scrutiny. It seemed as though the new government was especially interested in cracking down on any security risks connected with the country's nuclear program. His father warned that he could at least expect to be severely beaten if he returned home. Legally speaking, he could be prosecuted for divulging state secrets or for antistate activities, both charges punishable in a military court.

As time dragged on, Chaudhry remained in legal limbo, supporting himself by working in a convenience store. Our contact became more sporadic, and I could see his spirits were falling. As he put it in one email, "Life is getting terrible for me day by day." He seemed to have no future in the United States, but what was his alternative? "Go back to Pakistan and spend the rest of my life in Pakistani military jails." With the events of September 2001 and the heightened anti-Muslim feeling, he found his situation even more precarious. Lacking any legal documentation, he felt that any sort of travel had become dangerous.

Then came another blow to his hopes when his asylum claim was rejected early in 2002. According to the INS, "[you were] unable to satisfactorily establish your claimed identity as a highly placed nuclear scientist. Further it has been determined from a field investigation that several of the documents that you submitted in support of your claim appear to have been fraudulently produced. This includes the letters from your alleged former professor and medical doctor."

His only hope was to go before an immigration judge, and a date was set for a court appearance in New York City. However, Chaudhry felt this was not a good idea both for financial and personal security reasons. After getting our help to draft a request for a change of venue to a nearby city, he ended his connection with us. This, I'm afraid, is a fairly common situation in the immigration field. Like old soldiers, clients have been known to fade away. In our last communication, Chaudhry seemed to be weighing his chances of getting immigration sponsorship in either Canada or Germany. I can only hope that he succeeded and remains safe.

This case raised more questions than answers. It may be easy—too easy—to shrug off Chaudhry as some sort of con man or fraud. But the fact remains that his passport lists him as working in the Pakistan Government Service. Although his grasp of physics seemed a little shaky, the factual information he gave the U.S. government was certainly more than an accountant in a toilet factory would know. He provided me with detailed diaries with very specific missile specifications and original documents, which were later authenticated. Years later investigative journalist Seymour Hersh, a Pulitzer prize winner, investigated his credentials for a profile, authenticating his claims. As I said at the time, "to take on a government as he has, you'd have to be crazy unless the charges were real."

Chaudhry certainly didn't enjoy any great rewards from his defection, and his life remained precarious. The government spent years trying to discount the story he told, but subsequent events tended to support the facts he'd revealed. In 2003, Libya's dictator, Muammar Gaddafi, attempted to normalize relations with Western nations. Part of this effort involved revealing Libya's secret attempts to acquire a nuclear weapon. It also brought Pakistan's role in nuclear proliferation to light. Dr. Abdul Qadeer Khan hadn't merely managed to build a bomb, he had pioneered the way for a country without a lot of high tech to outsource the creation of a nuclear weapon. Blueprints for bombs, blueprints for the centrifuges needed to concentrate the fissionable material, even tips for finding tech companies in countries such as Malaysia to do the necessary nuts-and-bolts work—all could be found in the Pakistani Bomb Bazaar.

Did Khan profit from these transactions? Undoubtedly. But this was no individual effort. Pakistan received shipments of oil from Iran in return for nuclear know-how. It received aid in developing long-range missiles from North Korea when Khan visited that country to help develop weapons-grade uranium. In 2004, Khan, the father of Pakistan's A-bomb, made a tearful confession on national Pakistani television that he had embarrassed his homeland by selling nuclear knowledge and technology to North Korea, Libya, and Iran. The Pakistani government promptly pardoned him, although they placed him under house arrest for four years. Khan subsequently denied his confession.

As for Iftikhar Khan Chaudhry, I can only hope he's in the wind somewhere.

— 9 —

The Heartbroken Mothers

Desiring to protect children internationally from the
harmful effects of their wrongful removal or retention . . .
as well as to secure protection for rights of access.

—*Preamble to the Hague Abduction Convention*

One of the primary goals of immigration law is the reunifica-
tion of families. As an immigration lawyer, one of the most painful parts
of my practice involves representing parents when they attempt to recover
their children after estranged spouses kidnap them and take them to
foreign countries.

The United States is a nation of immigrants, and according to the last
census, one in five marriages has a foreign-born partner. Unfortunately,
the United States is also notorious for having a high divorce rate—people
often say as high as 50 percent. They get that number by comparing the
number of divorces in a particular year against the number of marriages.
Divorce is rarely pleasant and is often contentious, leading some spouses
to take extreme measures. Here's another sad statistic: the United States

has the highest number of international child abductions in the world today. This is not a new crime—it's been going on as long as there have been borders. The book of Genesis tells the story of the patriarch Jacob, who, after some difficulties with his father-in-law, Laban, left the land of Aram for Canaan with his two wives (Laban's daughters) and his children. Laban pursued, and the situation was settled amicably.

For thousands of years, the problem of a disaffected spouse taking children to another country has revolved around a difficult question, "Which country's laws should cover the situation?" The Hague Convention of 1961 attempted to create a multilateral framework to address the question, with ninety-seven countries presently agreeing on the prompt return of children wrongfully removed. That can still require considerable legal effort in foreign courts and sometimes heartbreak as a court sides with a native-born spouse. Still worse, however, is the fact that many countries, especially those in the Middle East, refuse to sign this agreement. Children are considered citizens of these countries, and mothers often have no rights at all.

In 1994, I had helped a Saudi diplomat, Mohammed al-Khilewi, defect from Saudi Arabia. Then Pat Roush approached me with further evidence of Saudi corruption. By that time, almost eight years had passed since her husband had kidnapped their children and taken them to Saudi Arabia. She met her husband in college. Roush was an older student just spreading her wings and opening herself to new things. One of those new things was Khalid al Gheshayan, one of numerous young Saudi nationals sent to study in the United States. Although not an outstanding student—he failed or withdrew from all but two of the courses he took over four years—he was charming, attentive, and persistent. They married in 1978, and Roush soon gave birth to a baby girl, Alia. But Gheshayan's drinking put a strain on the family, especially when he was arrested for drunk driving, battery, and vandalism. He also had mental problems and was diagnosed as a paranoid schizophrenic who also suffered from acute and chronic alcoholism and alcoholic hepatitis.

By 1981, Gheshayan had been going back and forth between San Francisco and Riyahd for several years, living away from Roush and Alia even when in San Francisco. Roush tried desperately to be free of him, working and taking care of Alia. She had graduated from San Francisco State University with a degree in anthropology and had a lovely apartment with Alia. In 1981 Gheshayan returned to California with his father, a powerful Saudi businessman, very well connected to the royal family. Gheshayan convinced Roush that he was in business with his father, had totally changed, and wanted to be a good father to Alia. She trusted him and gave birth to their second daughter, Aisha, in 1982. But he hadn't changed, and Roush told him to leave. She went back to school and studied nursing in San Francisco, living happily with her little girls. In her third year of nursing school, Roush became very ill and had to quit school just months before graduating from the course. She couldn't work or go to school.

Gheshayan told her he and his family could help, but she and the children had to come to Saudi Arabia where she could recover her health. She found the closed, repressive Saudi society to be an Arabian nightmare—and then she discovered she couldn't leave! By Saudi law, a woman is under the guardianship of her male relations. Roush couldn't depart from the country without her husband's permission. After much persuasion, she managed to get herself and the girls back to the United States, and she commenced divorce proceedings. She gained sole custody of Aisha and Alia. Gheshayan followed them to the United States, and Roush allowed him visitation rights with the little ones.

On the second visit, Gheshayan absconded with the children to Saudi Arabia. That was in 1986. Alia was seven. Aisha was three. Then the Arabian nightmare began in earnest. Roush discovered that her custody order and arrest warrants from U.S. courts meant nothing in her husband's homeland. The fact that she still fought for her children—and persisted for years—seemed to infuriate the Saudis. In their eyes, she was a mere woman with no rights. How dare she speak out? Even more annoying, Roush brought the topic of international child abduction and the Saudis' shameful record on the subject into the full glare of publicity. She is truly a pioneer in the movement. Until she brought up the topic with Senator Alan Dixon, the United States hadn't even signed onto the Hague Convention.

As a father myself, I couldn't imagine anything worse than to have held my daughters as babies and not be able to hold them as they grow older. I tried to use my media contacts and the connections I'd made in

Saudi Arabia to negotiate a settlement that would get the girls out of the country. But as happened all too frequently on this long, long journey, the resolution slipped between our fingers, often undermined by our own State Department. Too many of our diplomats seemed to regard the Saudis as their clients rather than fighting for Roush's cause. Our government seemed to operate on a skewed set of priorities. They will send in a SWAT team to resolve a politically charged family custody case for a Cuban child such as Elián González but ignore the needs of more than 11,000 young Americans kidnapped to foreign countries. As I said in a television interview, "The American government cares more about its oil and its military agenda than its daughters."

In 1995, almost ten years after this struggle began, Roush had two hours in a Riyadh hotel room with her daughters, now young women. Alia spoke English with an Arab accent, but Aisha had lost her English altogether. She didn't even know her birth date because Muslims don't celebrate birthdays. Roush had no other further contact with her daughters until 2003, and then visited them again in 2005. Aisha succeeded in fleeing the country and has lived with her mother for the past nine years. Alia, at long last, is also able to visit. At the age of seventy-one, three decades after her children were stolen, Roush has a family again—including eight grandchildren—but a long, bitter history with her government.

According to State Department and U.S. law enforcement, in international affairs criminal cases take a back seat to civil cases. The effort of tracking down a kidnapper and victims is considered a "private legal matter between parents." During my association with Roush, we spent a lot of time in Washington, making noise but also helping to make law. Results include getting an international children's abduction law passed in Congress and the establishment of an Office of Children's Concerns in the State Department. That gave us some additional tools for other cases.

When Mary Huber, an American girl, met a Palestinian-American boy, Mohamad Hamouda, at his parents' pizza parlor in Maryland, it seemed like a case of love and marriage. They had three young children, but ended up separating in June 1999. Mary Hamouda took out an order of protection against her husband. When it expired, Mohamad arranged for the children, Ashley (ten), Alexandra (six), and Amanda (four), to make an overnight visit to his parents' house.

Instead, he headed off with the children to southern Lebanon, then controlled by Israel. Mary tried to get a warrant for Mohamad's arrest from Maryland officials but lost precious days when they insisted she needed a court order showing that she had sole custody. When she returned with that, police told her it was invalid because she'd gotten it after her spouse had absconded. In fact, even in a shared custody arrangement, a spouse cannot act unilaterally in respect to the children. The other spouse must be notified. As in many international abduction cases, law enforcement is often ignorant of the legal aspects. The local police tended to treat Mary's case as a domestic dispute. Even the FBI was initially slow to respond despite the fact that the area where Hamouda took the children was a conflict zone and 256 Israeli servicemen were killed over the course of the conflict.

Mary frantically contacted every agency she was referred to, including P.A.R.E.N.T. International, an advocacy group founded by Maureen Dabbagh, who was a pioneer in the international child abduction movement. They, in turn, contacted me. Mary approached me after I spoke at a Abduction Conference in Washington, DC; she was holding a homemade flyer she had crafted with photos of her three girls. By tracing the children's passports, we learned that Mohamad had taken them to Switzerland and then to Lebanon, where he had lived as a small child. Thanks to some prodding from the State Department, we got the FBI to issue a federal arrest warrant under the international child kidnapping law for which Pat Roush and I had campaigned. An interesting side note to this case is that even though it involved international kidnapping both parents were U.S. citizens. Mohamad was in Lebanon on a visitor's visa.

My inquiries revealed a turf war. The FBI claimed it was a local police matter, and the local police department pointed a finger to the FBI! Over a cup of coffee with Mary, it dawned on me that her brother-in-law had driven the girls to the airport, presenting himself as an accomplice and setting the stage to leverage the brother's criminal prosecution in return for the girls' return. It took several months, but we successfully arranged a sting operation that brought Mohamad and the children back to the United States. He was arrested, and the children were returned to their mother. Getting all three back was quite a feat, as I had feared the father would leave one daughter behind as a bargaining chip. Mohamad pleaded guilty. I was glad for the resolution, but it was unbelievable to me that law enforcement has very limited tools to use to retrieve these children once they are spirited abroad. Case by case, we see those laws changing.

Even in a country that has signed on to the Hague Convention, child abduction can be a torturous business. Consider the case of Rachel Drai, who left France with her husband after his bankruptcy and legal problems forced him from his home in Marseilles in 1998. After an unsuccessful job search in Israel, Bernard Drai came to the United States, where he found employment with an Israeli educator raising funds in this country. Rachel took on secretarial work for the rabbi's organization as well. She also had a child, Ahuva Lieva, in 1999.

Fits of violence on Bernard's part and the accusation of misappropriating funds strained the marriage. Early in 2000, when Rachel had to travel to Los Angeles for work reasons, Bernard absconded with the two youngest children, Ahuva Lieva and Chaya. Once in Marseilles, he telephoned his wife, demanding that she come to his family home. As a way to put pressure on her, he contacted the U.S. embassy to cancel his family's visas to stay in the United States. Because he was no longer working in this country, the visas, good until 2002, would be invalid. Rachel received a notice that the Chief Rabbi of France had been requested to negotiate an agreement for the estranged couple. When she came to Paris, her husband never appeared at the rabbi's office. Instead, he turned up in New York, attempting to removed his other three children from their school, only to be thwarted by the school principal. When Rachel turned to New York City Councilman Noach Dear for help, he referred her to me. There were two parts to this case. Rachel went to family court for custody, and I dealt with the visa issue.

The family court nearly refused to accept jurisdiction on the matter—neither Rachel's attorney nor the legal secretary of the court had a firm understanding of the international aspects of the law. In the end, however, we secured temporary custody of all five children for Rachel, along with an order of protection. The visa issue was resolved more easily. Rachel was teaching religious subjects, so I was able to get her an R1 visa for temporary employment in a religious capacity.

In addition, I notified the French police of Bernard's lawbreaking, which led to his arrest. The little girls would return to the United States with Rachel's mother. Unfortunately, the way still wasn't smooth. Chaya's visa had already been stamped "canceled," and Ahuva Lieva's U.S. passport had been destroyed. By quickly contacting our Paris embassy, I was able to get a replacement passport and arrange to have Chaya allowed into the United States even though she was technically "undocumented." On a personal note, I should add that all of this activity happened at the beginning of Passover, making for yet another memorable holiday.

This was another case in which the International Child Kidnapping Act played a part in bringing about a just resolution. I also appreciated the timely intervention of the late New York Congressman Ben Gilman in expediting Rachel's visa application.

Conclusion

All three of these cases might be said to have happy endings, but they certainly weren't pleasant experiences for those involved—especially for Pat Roush whose ordeal lasted for decades. Things have changed over thirty years. The State Department now has an Office of Children's Issues and has issued a twenty-six-page guide on international child abduction. Unfortunately, our diplomatic service inclines more toward maintaining good relations with other countries than maintaining the rights and even the safety of young citizens. In addition, our nation's law enforcement and even judicial personnel are woefully ignorant of the international aspects of parental abductions.

We need better knowledge, better laws, and better international relationships to protect children. As more and more marriages cross national and cultural boundaries, we face more, not fewer, possibilities for a vengeful parent absconding with a child in the course of a divorce. Spouses must learn to protect themselves, or they will find their children stolen away—and the children deprived of their childhood.

—10—

To Be Young, Ambitious, and a Target

This memorandum rescinds the June 15, 2012 memorandum entitled "Exercising Prosecutorial Discretion with Respect to Individuals Who Came to the United States as Children," which established the program known as Deferred Action for Childhood Arrivals ("DACA"). For the reasons and in the manner outlined below, Department of Homeland Security personnel shall take all appropriate actions to execute a wind-down of the program, consistent with the parameters established in this memorandum.

—*Memorandum on Rescission of Deferred Action for Childhood Arrivals*

You might consider Rezai Karim to be almost the poster boy for seeking the American Dream through immigration. Brought to this country as a five-year-old, he spent the next thirty years pursuing every opportunity for advancement, resulting in education, a good job, and even attempting to find a way to regularize his status.

On closer examination, you can see how precarious his story really was. Growing up in New York, it wasn't until high school that he realized the limitations being undocumented would put on his life. He had a hard time finding a job to support his ambition to go to college, finally finding a position at Dunkin' Donuts. The same cloud of uncertainty hung over life after college. Karim decided against pursuing a law career, unsure where he'd be able to get work. As he put it, "I couldn't do anything for myself."

In 2012, the government offered a glimmer of hope with the Deferred Action for Childhood Arrivals (DACA) program. Almost forty years before, my father had uncovered the arcane workings of deferred action in the immigration service through a series of actions under the Freedom of Information Act. The 2012 version of DACA was more straightforward. Immigrants who had arrived in the United States before the age of sixteen and were under thirty-one years of age at the start of the program could apply for work authorization and avoid deportation. There were drawbacks. The status had to be renewed every two years for a fairly hefty fee, and it didn't allow for any permanent change of status—not citizenship, not even residency. That didn't stop more than 800,000 young people from seeking DACA status. It allowed Karim to move to Roanoke, Virginia, and start a new job in the computer engineering field.

On August 20, 2016, the first day of moving into a new apartment, this success story turned into a horror show. Karim and a female companion were enjoying the pool in the residential complex when it began to rain. As Karim opened the door to his apartment, they were accosted by a stranger, Waqil Farooqui, who had been sitting in the stairwell, smoking a cigarette. Farooqui approached and Karim felt a sharp blow; he had been stabbed with a knife. As he fell to the floor, he heard his assailant cry, *"Allahu Akhbar!"*—"God is great!" Although his Muslim family is not religious, Karim knew that this phrase in private was a prayer, but in public it meant a terrorist attack. Fighting off unconsciousness, he forced himself back to his feet to confront his attacker, who had now turned his attention to the young lady.

In New York, Karim had been an amateur boxer, taking part in the Golden Gloves tournament. Now he was fighting for his life, biting his adversary and grabbing his wrist to wrestle for the knife. The couple managed to escape down the stairs and out of the building with Farooqui following, but he ran off into the night as Karim screamed for someone—anyone—to stop him. Only when Farooqui fled did Karim and his companion realize they were covered in blood. They collapsed as onlookers called for medical assistance. Police found a large amount of blood in the apartment and a bloody trail leading to the victims. Karim and the young woman were taken to the local emergency room. Karim had suffered a neck wound serious enough that some speculated the attack had been an attempt at an ISIS-style decapitation. For Karim it was enough that the slash was almost long enough to have severed his jugular.

A short time later their attacker appeared at the hospital asking for treatment for damage he'd received in the fight. He was quickly taken into custody and admitted his attack. Farooqui said he had left his home that evening to "clear his head." He took a large kitchen knife with him, and in the course of the evening, he had heard voices calling him stupid and urging him to attack people. He did not know Karim, having chosen him and his companion at random. Upon hearing this, Karim said perhaps it was better that he'd been chosen instead of some of the kids who had been at the swimming pool.

Farooqui, an American-born U.S. citizen, had a record of some traffic infractions and had appeared on the FBI's radar as a possible self-radicalized terror suspect. There's a rather grim saying in the news business—"If it bleeds, it leads." Gory stories tend to be played up, and beyond its gruesome aspects was the suggestion of terrorism. This was a case guaranteed to draw media attention, not just from the local newspapers but from the *Washington Post* and even the *Daily News* in New York. Various news sources reported that Farooqui had gone to Europe and made it as far as Turkey, perhaps in an attempt to reach Syria and the forces of ISIS. ISIS, however, did not claim responsibility for the attack, and Farooqui's lawyer claims that he had no contact with any organizations—that his actions were attributable to mental illness.

My office was already working for Karim to extend his DACA status, but now we would also have to manage the media—to find a balance between serving his immigration interests and protecting as much of his privacy as possible. He appeared in a *Newsweek* article about the attack, but we made sure his face was obscured in any photographs.

That attack also opened another possible legal avenue for Karim—the U visa. This program was established for crime victims who had suffered considerable physical or mental abuse due to crime and who assist law enforcement in prosecution. For many undocumented immigrants, it has become the equivalent of Willy Wonka's Golden Ticket—after three years, a person with a clean record and a U visa can apply for a green card, and five years after that, for naturalization as a citizen.

Like that mythical Golden Ticket, though, the U visa has become harder and harder to acquire. By law, only 10,000 U visas may be granted each year. Although the U visa was created in 2000, actual visas were not issued until 2009. In that year, almost 11,000 petitions for the status were received, and there was already a backlog of more than 21,000. The last full year for which we have records is 2016, when more than 30,000 petitions were received. The prospects are that 2017 petitions will exceed that number, with a present backlog of more than 135,000.

We had abundant proof that Karim had suffered severe physical injuries from Farooqui's attack. The question was prosecution. Remember the shoe bombing case? When Richard Reid was arraigned, he decided to plead guilty, and no prosecution was necessary. The federal authorities decided not to give Kwame James a U visa, although they had promised him they would do so when they were eager to make a case.

Farooqui was held without bond at the Western Virginia Regional Jail. A grand jury turned in an indictment in his case early in December 2016. Farooqui's lawyers were laying the groundwork for an insanity defense and arguing to have testimony about him shouting *"Allahu Akbar!"* barred from being mentioned in court. They did not succeed in having that testimony barred, and Farooqui ended up pleading guilty days before his trial was set to begin. He had been charged with two counts of aggravated malicious wounding, which is a Class 3 felony in the Commonwealth of Virginia, punishable by a prison sentence of up to twenty years and a $100,000 fine. At the final sentencing on January 18, 2018, Farooqui received sixteen years in prison.

In the meantime, we've also been working with federal prosecutors on a terrorism case for the attack. Although Farooqui's attorney insists that his mental state precipitated his actions, Farooqui had engaged in activities that brought him to the attention of the FBI. However, his case didn't represent any serious wrongdoing until his attack. No terrorist organization officially claimed responsibility for his deeds, but we would like to know whether he was influenced by any groups or whether he had self-radicalized in seeking to act out so violently.

Karim and his friend have healed after this bloody assault—at least physically. The young lady still suffers from panic attacks, and Karim has been winding down his job with an eye to returning to New York. Like it or not, he's had to admit that even the middle of Virginia isn't necessarily a safe haven anymore. A U visa has allowed for a relatively happy ending for Karim's immigration fears, but he is only one out of more than 800,000 young people left in limbo by the Trump administration's decision to terminate DACA.

The deferred action program was never supposed to be a final fix. It was to be a temporary measure in the expectation that legislative action such as the DREAM Act would pass Congress. Unfortunately, that didn't happen, and when President Obama tried to expand DACA, twenty-six states—both red and blue states—sued to block it. In the months since Donald Trump came to office, Texas, Alabama, Arkansas, Louisiana, Idaho, Kansas, Tennessee, South Carolina, Nebraska, and West Virginia—red states that have made significant moves against immigrants—have now sued to declare DACA unconstitutional.

I think it's bad public policy to promise rights to people and then yank them away. After all, the people we're talking about are young Americans. They speak English without accents and have only vague memories of the countries from which they came. Various states have invested in their futures, educating them, and now political factions want to reject them right when that investment is about to pay off. They don't care that 91 percent of DACA recipients are employed and that firing them would cause economic dislocation. Nor do they care that a number of these young people are serving in our armed forces. They'd rather waste all that human talent, not to mention the trust of a huge swathe of our population.

Many who signed up for DACA in hope now feel fear, wondering if they've only volunteered to put their names on deportation lists. It's a disheartening situation. The U visa program was designed to create better bonds between the immigrant community and law enforcement.

But for political reasons, in some localities law enforcement won't certify that immigrants are helping in cases. Programs that were started to find gang members and terrorists are instead being aimed at immigrants without criminal connections. And the continuing political tirades have only deepened the distrust in immigrant communities. In a 2008 survey, 50 percent of Hispanic immigrants felt just some or very little confidence that law enforcement would treat them fairly. Still, 78 percent said they would contact the police if they suffered a violent crime, and the percentage rose to 84 percent in the case of a property crime. In 2013, however, a full 44 percent of Latino immigrants felt they would be *less* likely to call the police as crime victims "for fear that they will ask me or people I know about our immigration status." There have been no large-scale surveys since the advent of the Trump administration, but several cities with large immigrant populations have recorded significant drops in the number of crime reports from immigrant-heavy neighborhoods.

It can't be a good idea to encourage crime in any neighborhood. There's no guarantee that a criminal who preys on immigrants won't also attack other citizens. Nor is it good in the long term for a nation even to consider driving away productive citizens. For most of the twentieth century, the United States benefited as the recipient of a "brain drain" from Europe, and no nation that drove off large amounts of its human capital did well. Once Czarist Russia, Nazi Germany, and the former Soviet bloc were powerful entities. Each in its way drove millions of young, educated, and entrepreneurial citizens to leave. Is it really wise to follow that example?

—11—

The Spies Who Loved One Another

The S nonimmigrant classification is generally available
to aliens who would otherwise be inadmissible to or
deportable from the United States (for example, due to
criminal convictions or certain problems with immigration
status). The statute authorizes the Secretary of Homeland
Security to waive most grounds of inadmissibility. The
program is particularly useful for witnesses or informants
who would otherwise be in danger in their home countries.
It is also a substantial benefit for many other witnesses and
informants who might not otherwise be able legally to
enter or remain in the United States.

—*S Visa Program—Eligibility*

When the Soviet Union fell in 1991, there were high hopes for the victory of democracy and an end to the Cold War. But there were a lot of unintended consequences. The new Russian government managed to be both ineffective and authoritarian. Attempts to institute a free market economy led to much privation and the rise of oligarchs taking over formerly state-run enterprises. Organized crime ran rampant. Outside observers started referring to the Russian Federation in terms of the lawlessness and wildcat capitalism of the old Wild West.

It was against this chaotic background that young Alexei Artamonov grew up, pursuing a career in the family business—state security. Both his parents worked for the KGB, his grandfather was an intelligence officer who interrogated prisoners in World War II, and his great-grandfather had been part of the Czarist secret police. The service Artamonov entered was a far cry from the KGB of the Soviet era, which had spied on foreign nations—and also on citizens at home. That agency was dismantled, and the FSB (*Federal'naia sluzhba bezopasnosti* or Federal Security Service) was tasked with counterintelligence, border protection, counterterrorism, and investigation of federal law violations. In American terms, the FSB covers the territory of the FBI, Immigration and Customs Enforcement (ICE), Homeland Security's Federal Protective Service, the National Security Agency (NSA), Customs and Border Protection, the Coast Guard, and part of the turf of the Drug Enforcement Administration. Although its officers don't wear uniforms, the FSB is a military operation, and Artamonov rose to the rank of captain. He even met his wife through the service.

In addition to all its official duties, however, the FSB does some very important work off the books, providing *krysha*, literally a "roof"—cover for corruption and help in the transit and laundering of dirty money. Even before the rise of the oligarchs, black markets and corruption had been a regular feature of Soviet life. But the wide-open days of the nineties poured vast amounts of cash into a crooked system, and as political figures demanded their cut, they created a kleptocracy—government by thieves, for the thieves, and to the detriment of the national budget and economy. *Cherny Nal*, "black cash," is sent to the financial centers in St. Petersburg or Moscow in enormous amounts. Ruble notes are shipped in cargo planes by weight from the big operators, and smaller operations deliver duffel bags full of cash by car.

Artamonov's father foresaw a career in foreign intelligence for his son, sending him at the age of seventeen to the FSB academy, or "KGB high school." Even before that, Artamonov had been sent to New York and

Miami as an exchange student, to get to know the enemy and the enemy's language. Instead, Artamonov discovered he rather liked the enemy. "It was completely different than Russia," he was to say later, "an open world."

The plan to have an international spy in the family went off the rails when Artamonov married his first wife—from outside the KGB. He graduated with a master's degree in criminal law, and as a newly minted second lieutenant was sent to the counterintelligence side of state security, working financial crimes. Promotions came slowly, and Artamonov began to feel his career had stalled. He also saw golden opportunities in the private sector. As a financial watchdog, he'd already accepted bribes. It was pretty much an accepted system. As Artamonov put it, "Law enforcement agencies, intelligence, court system, government officials, business and criminal families have deeply integrated into each other and have organized as one large criminal syndicate."

Everyone was out to get rich quick, and Artamonov went where the real money was, becoming deputy head of security at Creditimpex Bank. The name would suggest an import-export connection, but by 2005 the bank was mainly exporting billions, laundering money and moving it offshore. A big concern in a kleptocracy is keeping one's ill-gotten gains from being stolen by a larger crook. He knew where the money was coming from: "tax evasion, concealment of illegal profit, bribery, hiding real beneficiaries, legalization of dirty money, and corruption." After playing a shell game with *odnodnevki* and *pomoiki*, literally "ephemeral" and "trash," companies, cash arrived at the bank and went out for fake loans or reinvestment schemes in Malta, Vietnam, the British Virgin Islands, and the Baltic states, where it would be parked or laundered.

Artamonov could make tens of thousands of dollars a month in fees, or "gratitude," in addition to his regular salary. Similar gratitude ensured an "eyes closed policy" from the government. FSB contacts not only warned when an investigation might begin but participated in physically transporting money. In such a climate of greed, it was inevitable that Artamonov would overreach. "We got too greedy," Artamonov admitted, and his associates turned on him. "The first I knew my bank accounts were frozen. Then the threats came." His father called to warn that the only choice to resolve the situation was "the officer's way"—to shoot himself—or his associates would do the job for him. Instead, Artamonov went for a third alternative, to flee for his life. He and his wife Victorya left Russia for the Dominican Republic, one of the few places that didn't require a visa for people with a Russian passport and was out of the direct reach of the government. They left their savings and their lives behind.

As far as Artamonov's parents were concerned, he had become an Enemy of the State, and a tremendous number of people who received that title ended up dead. In Russia, Serge Magnitsky, an auditor, discovered a huge tax fraud orchestrated by high police officials. He wound up being accused of the crime he'd uncovered and died in custody. Boris Berezovsky, the billionaire who had financed Vladimir Putin's rise to power, fell out with the Russian leader, fled to London, and spent years propagandizing against Putin, only to end up deceased with an unproven cause of death. Alexander Litvinenko, a former FSB officer who defected with information about criminal corruption, was poisoned with radioactive polonium, suffering a lingering, painful death.

As exiles, Artamonov and Victorya faced a precarious future unless they came up with a Plan B. In the end they approached the U.S. embassy, offering information to the CIA. The idea was to trade Artamonov's knowledge of connections between banks and criminal operations both in Russia and in the United States for a comfortable sum of money and a foreign passport to settle in Denmark or Switzerland.

Instead, after initially interrogating Artamonov and Victorya, the CIA transferred the couple to the FBI. A supposed island-hop to Puerto Rico turned into a trip to the U.S. mainland. Still, the prospects seemed good—the FBI offered a payment of $300,000 and a contract offering $7,000 a month for assisting with investigations. According to Artamonov, "The FBI assured us we would receive passports, social security cards, driver's licenses. That we would get certified copies of our Russian qualifications to use in the United States so we could find jobs. The Virginia FBI office said we could have a green card within a year if we cooperated." The Artamonovs can't talk about the specifics of their work for the FBI—their contract obligates them not to disclose anything. But for five years, they helped the feds make headway against Russian mafia operations and money laundering in this country.

During that time, Artamonov went before a judge to change his name—to Janosh (for Janus, the god of beginnings and endings) Neumann (a "new man"). However, relations with the FBI became contentious. Neumann would give information only on illegal FSB activities. "I never set up anyone from the Russian intelligence," he insists. His targets were "gangsters, criminals, guys who are dirty, guys who are corrupted." Complaints circulated that his manner was arrogant. Certainly, he was not impressed with the U.S. security services. He mentions that their first CIA contact wore a wig that needed constant adjusting. As for the FBI, he compared it to "a second-rate soccer team."

By this time, the Neumanns had been brought to Portland, Oregon. As Neumann puts it, "This is not at all what we imagined when we went to the Americans. We don't have jobs, we don't have documents. We live in a place we never even heard of before we got here." As undocumented foreigners, they had to pay a premium for everything. It was prohibitively expensive to find housing. And simple stress had taken a toll on Victorya's health, to the tune of more than six figures in medical expenses.

But they did their jobs, working undercover to identify financial misdoing and smuggling aided and abetted by Russian security agencies such as the SVR (foreign intelligence) and GRU (military intelligence) whose work with organized crime groups dates back to the days of the old Soviet bloc, "using them in their interest," Neumann explains, "specifically for dirty work and legalization of dirty money." Despite blowing the whistle, naming names, uncovering corrupt schemes, and the fact that to his former security colleagues "I'm already dead," Neumann still loves his homeland. "I defected from the system, not my country," he insists.

After five years of service, the worst happened. The FBI ended the Neumanns' contracts, which also meant an end for their visas as people cooperating with federal law enforcement. Neumann and Victorya no longer had Russian passports but could no longer stay in the United States. They had become people without a country and were exposed to retaliation from the criminal types they had exposed. When they attempted to apply for asylum, the immigration service rejected their appeal on the grounds that they were dangerous foreign agents. In other words, the experience that had made them invaluable to national security was used against them. As Neumann recalls his initial meeting with the

FBI, "One of the first things they asked was, did you kill anyone? I was clear. No, never."

One of the murkier issues revolved around torture, where Neumann's command of English may have let him down. During the asylum interview, he was asked, "Are you doing anything physical? I said, not by myself. It's not my job to do so. Of course, I know how this looks like. I know how to do this. But I never do this by myself." To some, that sounded as though he asked questions during an interrogation and left the dirty work to others. Neumann and his wife insist that is not what he meant, but the interview ended disastrously. They lost their bid for asylum.

This result did not sit well with some of their more sympathetic contacts in the FBI. Even though Neumann and Victorya had stirred up a hornet's nest by threatening to sue the bureau and by giving a long interview to a British newspaper, the *Guardian*, colleagues thought they hadn't received their due. Maybe it was too much to hope for the splashy lifestyle that Hollywood painted for defectors. But Neumann and Victorya seemed to be living the American Nightmare—wrecked credit, crippling medical bills, foreclosure—and now they would just be kicked out of the country.

I have to admit, I found it very ironic when the FBI reached out to me with an official request for my services. Years before, a similar but unofficial approach had earned an internal investigation for the FBI agents who'd asked for my help. Times had certainly changed—the FBI was even talking about paying for my services. Although that notion evaporated, I could see that I was the last, desperate hope for this couple. The Neumanns were in a difficult legal position, going before an immigration judge for deportation proceedings. I faced a prolonged campaign of litigation and negotiation. From a legal standpoint, when the Neumanns were first brought to the United States by the CIA, they should have qualified for the PL-110 program, essentially witness protection for defectors, with asylum, security, and even living expenses covered. Failing that, they should have received an S visa, for aliens assisting law enforcement, from the FBI. It seems as though the Neumanns represented a turf dispute between the two agencies, and their most important need seemingly never was addressed. Since the Neumanns were no longer officially cooperating with the FBI, the grounds for an S visa were no longer available. Add in another layer of bureaucracy from the U.S. Customs and Immigration Service and the mess became even more intractable. Even when Senator Ron Wyden, a member of the Intelligence Committee, started asking questions, he couldn't make any progress.

Neumann was frankly astonished at the situation. In Russia, state security is paramount. FSB officers could slash through red tape—and even laws—to achieve a security goal. In Neumann's view, the government agencies had made false representations to him—fraud—and then trapped him in this country—unlawful imprisonment. Needless to say, the FBI was not eager to engage in a legal dispute. Not only would it be embarrassing for the bureau, but it would also be bad for business. Publicizing the case could well deter potential defectors with important information. Worse, it would reveal the FBI's methods and procedures for helping people to defect, and even expose agents in place to danger.

The FBI was willing to play hardball, however, intimating that Victorya's health history might be revealed in court, affecting her chances for employment. The bureau had obtained the Neumanns' personal documents, passports, diplomas, and IDs for verification and had never returned them. Now, at last, they turned them over to me, with a written warning saying, in part, "acceptance of the attached materials may adversely impact the personal safety of Janosh Neumann and/or Victoria Neumann." In addition, "the United States Government denies any responsibility or liability for the personal safety of Janosh Neumann and/or Victoria Neumann." That was certainly a shift from the opinion I'd been given at the outset of my involvement in the case. When I'd asked if the Neumanns were in danger, I was told, "there is a substantial risk, but it may be mitigated by time."

In fact, with the revelations in the *Guardian*, the FSB showed it had not forgotten about its former operative. Instead of a treason charge, they went with bank fraud, claiming that Neumann had misappropriated a million and a half dollars. This Neumann dismisses as "a total lie," an attempt to discredit him, pointing out that Creditimpex Bank lost its license in 2015, its owners officially called money launderers and criminals—although they continue to do business, apparently under FSB protection.

My job was to secure a safe residency in this country for the Neumanns, by suggesting strategies and guiding negotiations between Neumann's and Victorya's lawyers, the FBI, and ICE, with the help of Senator Wyden's office. We succeeded in getting asylum for Victorya and a Grant of Deferral of Removal for Neumann. Thus, Neumann, Victorya, and their baby son will stay in this country. Both have received authorization to work, and Victorya has a clear path to permanent residency. Once she gets her green card, she can apply for a change in Neumann's status.

After such a complicated resolution, I have to admit surprise at the sequel—a group of retired military and covert operatives has joined together in a fund-raiser for the Neumanns. Former Navy SEAL Michael Janke has offered Neumann and Victorya jobs as consultants for his film production company and is even arranging for housing in California. Neumann had previously found some TV work in Portland, appearing as a Russian heavy in the supernatural drama *Grimm*. Neumann appreciates the help, and the reason for it. "They are doing this for their country, for what they believe is right. They are fixing the mistakes of others who failed to do their jobs in the first place."

I can understand some of his bitterness. To stick your neck out and come to a strange country in hopes of fighting corruption is hard enough. But when your newfound land can't—or won't—keep its promises, that must be a crushing blow. Worse, it has a chilling effect on others who might hope to trade important information for asylum in this country. Anyone willing to take possibly fatal risks to bring us warnings or intelligence should be welcomed vigorously, not confronted with an impassable line of bureaucrats. The Neumanns' case may not show our treatment of defectors in a very flattering light, but it should be an object lesson for the future on how to show honest gratitude and project a strong message to other people out there who would want to help America's homeland security issues here and abroad.

—12—

Looking Ahead

It's our right as a sovereign nation to choose immigrants
that we think are the likeliest to thrive and flourish
and love us.

—*President Donald J. Trump, September 1, 2017*

Today it is slightly more than a year since the inauguration of a new administration in Washington—and the announcement of a travel ban barely a week later. It took the Trump administration three iterations on this ban and six months before the Supreme Court allowed even partial implementation. Full implementation didn't come until December 2017. The initial travel ban faced considerable criticism essentially for being an attempt to keep Muslims out of the United States. On the third try, two non-Muslim nations were added: North Korea and Venezuela. The lineup for the latest targeted nations are Chad, Iran, Libya, North Korea, Syria, Venezuela, Somalia, and Yemen. Sudan had been included in the previous ban, but it was removed and replaced with Chad. Of course, North Korea has been in the diplomatic deep freeze from the beginning of the new administration, with inflammatory rhetoric between President Trump and "Dear Leader" Kim Jong-un flying higher than the North Korean dictator's ICBMs. The restrictions on Venezuelan nationals are aimed mainly at individuals in government and their families. Even with these additions, the ban is considered basically a religiously inspired one, and it remains in litigation.

As to the other campaign promises on immigration, the border wall is still in the prototype stages, and the price has risen to some $25 billion. The money for this strong southern border has become politically entangled with the fate of the young people in the DACA program, which was officially rescinded. So far, the situation has managed to generate one government shutdown, with a resolution supposed to be generated by Congress in the coming months. As with so much when it comes to immigration, we'll have to see how any legislation fares.

The administration has been quick to remove temporary protected status for some 60,000 Haitians living and working in the United States after a devastating 2010 earthquake. The same step was taken against 262,500 Salvadorans who came to this country on humanitarian grounds after two earthquakes rocked their homeland in 2001. The number of deportations has risen, not merely for Mexicans and Central American migrants (the major targets) but 24 percent for the rest of the world.

Since his reasoned statements on studying a number of issues during his confirmation hearings, Attorney General Jeff Sessions has taken a hard line in office. In addition to promoting the Trump agenda on immigration and opioids, Sessions has essentially declared a war against marijuana, even as many states have legalized various aspects of use for the drug.

What has that got to do with immigration? In April 2017 then-head of Homeland Security John Kelly enunciated a policy of actively enforcing the statutes against marijuana—and using those arrests to deport immigrants, legal and illegal, found with even small amounts of the drug. (Shades of John Lennon!) Though the Supreme Court has ruled that possession of small amounts for "social sharing" should not be considered an aggravated felony, encouraging prosecutorial discretion, the DHS juggernaut has proceeded to deport thousands on nonviolent pot charges, which the Obama administration had left alone. Looking to the future, we can expect contentious and difficult legal debate still to come.

A Question of Preemption

I expect that an important element in the ongoing debate will be the legal principle of preemption—that is, a federal law enacted through Congress overruling any conflicting laws of a lower authority. This has already begun to affect the enforcement of our immigration law—or rather, who's going to do the job. State and local governments have tried to supplement the shortcomings in federal immigration law for some time. One such measure has been ICE ACCESS agreements under section 287(g) of the Immigration and Naturalization Act (INA). ACCESS is an acronym for "Agreements of Cooperation in Communities to Enhance Safety and Security," and ICE is the acronym for Immigration and Customs Enforcement. In this series of agreements, thirteen combined programs are authorized to use local criminal justice systems—courts, jails, and police forces—to apprehend and confine people considered to be "criminal aliens." With these agreements, state and local law enforcement agencies can carry out immigration law functions that they would otherwise not be allowed to perform. I believe this will lead to more legal problems, with state and local governments wrestling with new and unfamiliar responsibilities or being persuaded that they need to impose more stringent immigration laws. Inevitably, this will mean conflict—and raise the specter of preemption.

It has long been established that the federal government is the supreme authority with respect to immigration, so state and local laws must clear two forms of preemption: Express Preemption and Implied Preemption. When a statute explicitly states that it preempts state or local laws, that's Express Preemption. This also occurs when there's a constitutional provision expressly delegating legislative functions with respect to a given arena to the feds—also known as Constitutional Preemption.

Examples of Implied Preemption include Conflict Preemption, when there's a direct conflict between a federal and state or local law so that enforcement of the state or local law would stand as an obstacle to the complete fulfillment of Congress's objectives. There's also Field Preemption, wherein Congress intended a complete ouster of state or local power to legislate a particular subject. Thus, even in the absence of a direct conflict between a federal and state or local law, the state or local law may be preempted.

In the case of *DeCanas v. Bica* the Supreme Court back in 1976 developed a three-step analysis for determining a California labor law:

1. Determine whether the state or local law/policy regulates immigration. If so, it's preempted.
2. Determine whether Congress has manifested a clear intent to oust states or localities from regulating the particular area of the state or local law/policy. If so, it is preempted.
3. Determine whether the state or local law/policy stands as an obstacle to the full accomplishment of the objectives of Congress, or makes compliance with federal and the state or local law/policy impossible. If so, it is preempted.

The Court stated, a "regulation of immigration" is a statute determining who should or should not be admitted into the United States, and the conditions under which a legal entrant may remain." These are preempted.

In contrast, regulations merely having an impact on or affecting immigration—but not regulating it—are not preempted. The court upheld the validity of the California statute restricting employers from knowingly employing an alien not entitled to lawful residence in the United States. Significantly, the California statute adopted federal standards in imposing sanctions against employers who employed aliens lacking a federal right to employment. Thus, it did not frustrate federal objectives.

In 1982 the case of *Plyler v. Doe* involved a Texas law to bar the enrollment of children in public schools if they were not legally in the United States. The Supreme Court struck down the law, but the decision stated, "States do have *some* authority to act with respect to illegal aliens, at least where such action mirrors federal objectives and furthers a legitimate state goal" (emphasis added). Moreover, the Immigration Reform and Control Act (IRCA) provides, "The provisions of this section preempt any State or local law imposing civil or criminal sanctions (other than through licensing or similar laws) upon those who employ . . . unauthorized aliens." The underlined portion is commonly referred to as the "Savings Clause."

The march of technology has simply made the matter even more contentious. E-Verify is an Internet-based system employers can use to verify an employee's work authorization. It allows an employer to submit a verification request and receive either a confirmation or a tentative nonconfirmation (TNC). If a TNC is issued, an employer must notify the employee, and the employee has eight days to challenge the initial finding. If an employee opts to challenge, a secondary verification process must be completed within ten business days. Should the employee fail to challenge the TNC or is unsuccessful in bringing a challenge, the employer must fire that employee or notify the Department of Homeland Security (DHS) that it will continue to employ the person. Failure to notify DHS will subject the employer to civil penalty and a presumption of having knowingly employed an unauthorized alien.

I hope readers will forgive what seems like a digression into the legal weeds. But I feel a thorough review of case law is required here to understand how the preemption doctrine has been applied—to predict how it may be implemented in the future.

In 2007, Arizona passed a law requiring all employers within the state to enroll in E-Verify. Under federal law, the program was voluntary. Arizona made E-Verify mandatory, and violations for noncompliance could result in permanent revocation of the employer's business license if committed during a specified probationary period. In the case of *CPLC v. Napolitano*, the Ninth Circuit Court upheld the validity of the law because it embodied federal standards and did not attempt to define who is eligible or ineligible to work under federal immigration laws.

On the other hand, in the *United States v. Illinois* the federal government challenged an Illinois law prohibiting employers from enrolling in E-Verify until determinations on 99 percent of TNC notices are issued to employers within three days. The reviewing district court held that the underlying federal interest in promoting E-Verify justified a finding of preemption insofar as the Illinois law frustrated federal objectives. (Thus fulfilling the third part of the *DeCanas v. Bica* test.)

Arizona's state legislature took action to promote the federal government's E-Verify program. This state action was upheld. Illinois's state legislature sought to restrict employers from utilizing E-Verify until the system met specified standards for accuracy and speed. This state action was preempted. The differing outcomes are suggestive of federal immigration laws/policies as a sort of immigration "low-water mark" or minimum.

In Nebraska the governor signed Legislative Bill 403, requiring public entities and contractors seeking public projects, and businesses qualifying for state tax incentive programs, to enroll in E-Verify. The bill also outlined the process by which state agencies could verify the eligibility of those applying for public benefits through the Systematic Alien Verification Entitlement (SAVE) program.

SAVE is a DHS program constituting a nationally accessible database of immigration status information on over sixty million records. SAVE is designed to examine an applicant's immigration status to ensure that only entitled applicants receive federal, state, or local public benefits. Assessing Nebraska LB 403 under *DeCanas v. Bica*, it is apparent that this is an instance of state action not preempted by federal immigration laws. Nebraska's implementation of E-Verify does not stand as an obstacle to the full accomplishment of Congress's objectives (*CPLC v. Napolitano*). SAVE is a program developed specifically for these circumstances.

The question of education and immigration continues with the case of *Equal Access Education v. Merton*. Virginia enacted a law prohibiting postsecondary education institutions from admitting people believed to have "illegal," "undocumented," or "unlawful" status within the meaning of federal law. The reviewing district court upheld the statute upon finding no conflict with federal immigration laws insofar as Virginia's statute incorporated federal standards in defining who would be ineligible for admission to state institutions. Outside the context of E-Verify, this holding supports the notion of federal standards serving as a low-water mark for immigration restrictions.

On the local law front, the city of Hazleton, Pennsylvania, enacted ordinances that sought to prohibit the harboring and employment of undocumented aliens by imposing penalties on landlords and employers. A harboring provision required occupancy permits that could only be obtained by U.S. citizens or lawful residents. The employment provision revoked employers' business licenses for hiring undocumented aliens and provided a private cause of action for lawful employees discharged while the employer maintained unlawfully present workers. Hazleton asserted that its ordinance constituted a licensing law valid under IRCA's Savings Clause.

The result was the case of *Lozano v. Hazleton* in 2005, in which the reviewing district court held that allowing Hazleton to revoke employers' business licenses, but not to impose civil or criminal sanctions, would only allow states to impose more severe forms of punishment. Thus, Hazleton's position was inconsistent with the purposes underlying IRCA. The court found that the "licensing" contemplated within IRCA referred only to revocation of licenses for IRCA violations, and not for violations of local laws. Thus, IRCA's Savings Clause was held entirely inapplicable to local ordinances.

The Hazleton ordinance defined "illegal alien" as "an alien who is not lawfully present in the United States according to the terms of United States Code Title 8, Section 1101." But Title 8, Section 1101 (commonly referred to as the Immigration Nationality Act) provides no definitions for the terms "illegal alien" or "lawfully present." The city sought to avoid preemption issues by "adopting federal standards" but failed to incorporate any actual federal standards. Hazleton's mayor and city council president explained the motivation behind Hazleton's ordinance as the result of the federal government's failure to address immigration problems, including the sudden appearance of muster zones, areas where day laborers collect in the morning to seek jobs. The visible presence of undocumented aliens often elicits strong and contentious debate among localities, resulting in pressure upon state and local officials to address immigration issues.

This brings us back to ICE ACCESS, which at least gives the impression of something being done about the immigrant problem. INA Section 287(g) envisions a cooperative framework under which federal and state or local authorities coordinate efforts to enforce federal immigration laws. But here's the problem: state and local governments have been forced to bear the increased costs of enforcing those laws—and these governments come to interpret their increased participation in enforcement of immigration laws as a cue to legislate immigration at a state or local level.

This can lead to a fracturing effect on law enforcement, as shown in *Louisiana v. Neri Lopez*. This case involved a Louisiana statute making it illegal for those unlawfully present to operate a motor vehicle. Louisiana's

Fourth Appellate Department held the state statute preempted by the federal REAL ID Act. Subsequently, however, Louisiana's First Appellate Department found no conflict between the statute and federal law. Thus, no preemption. The result is a jurisdictional split between Louisiana state courts and whether an individual is charged with illegally operating a motor vehicle while unlawfully present will depend upon fortuitous circumstances such as where one is apprehended by authorities.

As states and localities seek to take on a more active role in immigration, significant disparities between state and local immigration laws among and within states can be expected. Various levels of government will adopt ad hoc solutions to meet their individual needs, immigration law will lose its uniformity, and complicated nuances will eventually demand federal intervention. Rather than allowing complications to arise at the state and local level, the federal government ought to act to ensure comprehensive and uniform immigration reform. And it's got to be done soon. Several states and localities have made conscious efforts to avoid or disguise preemption issues. We can look forward to a lot of jousting over whether a state or local law frustrates federal immigration objectives.

Sanctuary Cities

Whatever the congressional objectives may be, the federal government does not have the resources to be omnipresent and ensure full enforcement. Although local government depicts itself as the first line of defense, in plain truth—it lacks jurisdiction to act.

In the case of *Muehler v. Mena*, the Supreme Court gave police officers full authority to request information pertaining to a person's immigration status. The Court explicitly equated that inquiry to the typical standard of questions asked to determine a person's name, address, and date of birth. By framing the inquiry that way, the question about a person's immigration status is brought outside of the scope of the Fourth Amendment. A law enforcement agent can delve into immigration status without fear of violating constitutionally protected rights. Questions regarding immigration status do not require a separate and distinct cause, which raises a reasonable suspicion. They are deemed appropriate even when a person cannot be legally searched or arrested.

However, not all states and cities are eager to hit the ground running. Some local and state governments have laws prohibiting their employees and law enforcement agents from disclosing information about an individual's illegal immigration status. Communities pass these laws because it leads to greater health and safety for the entire community. For example, when immigration status is not questioned, illegal immigrants are more likely to report crimes or to bring a sick family member to the emergency room.

We now see a number of large cities around the country, including New York City, prohibiting local law enforcement from making inquiries into an individual's immigration status at the initial stages of arrest. They borrowed the "don't ask, don't tell" policy from the military and applied it to law enforcement. It presented a simple solution: the state/city cannot notify the feds of that of which it is not aware. They cannot report someone's immigration status because they simply do not know it. However, even in New York City, an illegal immigrant, once convicted of a crime, is reported to immigration for possible deportation.

By creating a "safe haven" for undocumented aliens, cities that employ such practices came to be known as "sanctuary cities." The governments of these localities present myriad legitimate reasons for their practices. Some believe that aggressive measures against illegal immigrants would bluntly challenge the political structure of the federation, shaped for our country many years ago by its founding fathers. Others do not wish to create an adverse environment for illegal immigrant workers, whose diligent and often inexpensive labor is an indispensable part of their economy. Public policy is strongly in favor of sanctuary cities as well. Throughout our history, U.S. citizens have showed special sensitivity in matters regarding children. The laws passed to protect, educate, or help kids never discriminated against them based on the immigration status of their parents. Americans do not believe that children should suffer for the mistakes or immoralities of adults.

Sanctuary cities ensure that parents who entered the country illegally will send young children to elementary schools, and further education, without fear of deportation. They eliminate the moment of hesitation before calling a doctor for a sick child or taking an injured one to a hospital. That moment could be detrimental and, in many instances, life-threatening. Finally, a sanctuary city helps to control and detect criminal activity, which affects our youth and adults alike. In such an environment, individuals are not deterred from calling the police when witnessing criminal or suspicious activity.

New Jersey State Attorney General Anne Milgram issued Law-Enforcement Directive No. 2007-3 on August 22, 2007. This directive requires state, county, and local law enforcement agencies to alert federal authorities after arresting an undocumented immigrant for a serious offense. Specifically, all individuals arrested for indictable offenses under New Jersey State criminal law or for driving under the influence of alcohol will be questioned regarding their immigration status. This directive also indicates that victims, as well as witnesses and other persons requesting police assistance, should not be discouraged from approaching police officers out of fear of inquiry into their immigration status. The directive prohibits immigration status inquiries of victims and witnesses. This directive also prohibits local, county, and state law enforcement officials from performing functions of a federal immigration officer under Section 287(g) of the INA—or rather, it keeps them from exercising their federal immigration authority on anyone other than individuals arrested for serious indictable offenses and DUI. Officers working on immigration tasks forces under direct federal authority are exempt from this provision.

Many police chiefs in communities with significant immigrant and illegal immigrant populations do not wish to be deputized into enforcing federal immigration laws. Engaging in such enforcement erodes community policing efforts, uses limited police resources, and opens police departments to potential liability for unlawful arrests of documented immigrants and United States citizens. The United States Supreme Court allows local law enforcement to inquire into an individual's immigration status virtually at any given time. Most cities choose to prohibit such practices for public policy reasons: they do not wish to ask, and they don't wish to know.

Attorney General Sessions continues to warn about punitive moves against sanctuary cities, bringing the situation to a new boil recently when the Department of Justice sent out a letter threatening subpoenas against twenty-three jurisdictions with policies of not assisting federal immigration authorities. The letter demands information as to how these localities had instructed those in law enforcement with regard to how they should "communicate with the Department of Justice, the Department of Homeland Security, and/or Immigration and Customs Enforcement." The idea is to examine these instructions to make sure they agree with federal law. If they don't, federal funding will be cut for those jurisdictions. There's even some talk of trying to claw back funds from previous years. "We have seen too many examples of the threat to public safety represented by jurisdictions that actively thwart the federal government's immigration enforcement," the attorney general said when the wording in the letter was announced. "Enough is enough." This threatening letter was released on the same day that members of the U.S. Conference of Mayors were supposed to meet with the president to discuss rebuilding infrastructure. Several of the invited were mayors of sanctuary cities, and they declined to participate. On March 7, 2018, Sessions followed through, instituting a lawsuit against the entire state of California. For all his tough talk, however, the attorney general has not been able to implement his threats. A federal judge in Chicago ruled against Sessions in September 2017, and a San Francisco judge also blocked an executive order denying federal funding to sanctuary cities. This appears to be only the beginning of a long, drawn-out legal battle.

Across the country, there seems to be an interesting shift of opinion. A recent nationwide telephone and online survey found that 42 percent of likely U.S. voters think the U.S. Justice Department should take legal action against cities or states that provide sanctuary for illegal immigrants. That's down from 50 percent the year before, and 62 percent in 2015. An equal number (45 percent) felt the Justice Department shouldn't take legal action against these communities, up from 38 percent. Twelve percent weren't sure.

The kindest thing that can be said is that a vacuum has been created by congressional inaction. Once again, until Congress addresses this matter, immigrants will "vote with their feet," deciding where they choose to reside.

LGBTQ Concerns

When the Supreme Court struck down the anti–gay marriage provision in the Defense of Marriage Act (DOMA) in 2013, it opened a lot of doors for the lesbian, gay, bisexual, transgender, queer (LGBTQ) community. As Janet Napolitano, then head of the Department of Homeland Security put it, "President Obama directed federal departments to ensure the decision and its implications for federal benefits for same-sex legally married couples are implemented swiftly and smoothly. To that end, effective immediately, I have directed USCIS to review immigration visa petitions filed on behalf of a same-sex spouse in the same manner as those filed on behalf of an opposite-sex spouse."

Throughout the years, same-sex marriage has been a much-debated topic, and we can expect the debates to continue in various new forms. Many of those who support a liberal, democratic ideology believe all Americans should be entitled to full and equal benefits under the law as promised in the Fourteenth Amendment to the U.S. Constitution. The disparate treatment that has historically plagued the LGBTQ community has spurred outrage and blunt questions into the justifications for being treated as second-class citizens. Of course, this demand for equality has led to a more open dialogue on the question of citizenship in terms of immigration reform.

Overturning DOMA was an enormous victory for the LBGTQ community. With regard to immigration, the impact of this decision is that same-sex couples may file a green card application for the foreign national spouse. In addition, same-sex couples who petitioned for a green card years ago received a new opportunity for review of their cases. The policy went so far as to direct immigration officers that they may not require additional documents or information for applications filed by same-sex couples.

Society has been accustomed to seeing a mother, father, and their children as the standard American family. Yet shouldn't a family unit revolve around two loving and caring parents regardless of their sexes? The United States Census Bureau estimates that there were about 131,729 same-sex married couples in 2010, the last national census. Moreover, there were 515,735 same-sex unmarried couples. Clearly the idea of the nuclear family is evolving.

To turn from the theoretical to practical concerns, when filing an application for a same-sex couple, it must be shown that the marriage was entered into in good faith. This standard is universal and is applied to all couples. To ensure a smooth application process with the United States Citizenship and Immigration Service, couples should:

- Gather biographical data for both partners (i.e., the names, date, and place of birth of parents, present addresses, and employer information for the last five years).
- Secure access to all original documents such as both partners' original birth certificates, divorce decrees, if either was married before, or birth certificates of any children they have together.
- Open and use joint bank and credit card accounts. Keep copies of all statements.
- Collect photos of your life together, including your courtship, marriage, and other important occasions spent together such as holidays, birthdays, or vacations.

The improved marriage situation does not mean, unfortunately, that the process will be completely painless. The government has a tough job to do, reviewing the many applications and marriage records they receive each year. Experts will finely comb each petition they receive to determine whether the couple married for "love" or as a convenient way to help someone obtain immigration benefits. In addition, one must bear in mind that the existing state of affairs was affected by an executive order. With a new administration, changes may occur. Thus, although we keep the hope of change for the better, the prudent course is to seek the advice of immigration counsel regarding the latest developments in the field.

—13—

In Conclusion

We the People of the United States, in Order to form a
more perfect Union, establish Justice, insure domestic
Tranquility, provide for the common defence, promote the
general Welfare, and secure the Blessings of Liberty
to ourselves and our Posterity . . .

—Preamble to the U.S. Constitution

The fact that we have so many points of contention suggests that
our immigration system is broken. State governments and future admin-
istrations have to be aware that there is significant collateral damage from
political gridlock—we're working against our own best interests when we
make it impossible for the best and brightest foreign students to onboard
into U.S. companies. Essentially, that means we're just training them to
compete with us.

I think the present focus on immigration in the STEM segment of
the economy is shortsighted. Yes, science, technology, engineering, and
math are all important. But so are art, matters of the creative, and commerce. New York's fashion business, for example, puts 180,000 people
to work in some nine hundred companies and has a combined payroll of
$10 billion. Our economy has benefited by bringing in many risk-takers

and entrepreneurs from outside our borders. We need to reassess our treatment of foreign nationals at all stages, but especially students, to ensure that American businesses have the pick of the world's talent. We also have to make sure our regulations match the business environment. It completely perplexes me to learn that the H1B3 visa for fashion models is not available during fashion season.

Other countries have developed aggressive systems to secure foreign talent. The United State cannot afford to be passive in this world market—that's the road to marginalization. Our future governments at all levels must be in synch to bring foreign talent on board if we want to stay ahead of others. Inclusiveness fuels creativity, increases diversity in terms of gender and geographic background, and harnesses new business for the U.S. economy. As a mayor, I saw the local effects of a broken system—"stacking" of housing in urban centers; burgeoning muster zones for day laborers; financial burdens borne by taxpayers—yet the impetus for the federal government to do *something* remains low. The United States must act in a united manner to deal with the problem. I see this not merely as a business issue but as a matter of national security.

We must use immigration—the offer of a safe haven—as a weapon in today's chaotic world to attract the all-important human asset intelligence our law enforcement and national security agencies need to keep us safe. Eyes in the sky, whether satellites or drones, can only go so far. We need to create a fast track into our system for foreign diplomats, whistle-blowers, and well-intended human asset intelligence that is seamless and provides safety to those who would protect our interests—and their families.

Observers of Congress have said that the number of private immigration bills can serve as a barometer for how well the immigration system is working as a whole. The pitifully small number of such bills actually passed shows how even this court of last resort has become bogged down in politics. Some of this low output can be traced to reforms instituted some years ago after abuse of the system. But it boggled my mind that Kwame James, a foreign national who saved almost two hundred lives, couldn't find relief through Congress; whereas Michael Wilding, a British actor with a drug conviction, received this benefit. I'm not casting stones at Mr. Wilding. In some ways, his situation reminded me of my father's famous client, John Lennon. I'd like to believe that it's entirely beside the case that Mr. Wilding's mother was Elizabeth Taylor and his stepfather was Senator John Warner. Because if it requires a movie star and a senator to move Congress, we really have to take a hard look at our system.

America's Golden Doors require a good polishing and constant maintenance to protect us from danger. We must ensure that they will swing open wide in welcome to those who will benefit the democratic experiment envisioned by our founding fathers. Looking to the future, we never know who next will enter those gates to bring new vitality and discovery to the United States. Let us hope our legacy will be the excitement of opening doors rather than the insecurity of slamming them shut.

Appendix A

My Testimony to Congress on International Terrorism

On May 18, 1999, I appeared before the House Subcommittee on Immigration and the Claims Committee on the Judiciary two years before the 9/11 attacks.

Introduction

Good morning, Chairman Smith and Members of the Subcommittee. I am pleased to participate in this panel and present you with my initial assessments of Congressman Andrews' bill regarding the deportation of aliens who associate with known terrorists.

By way of background, I was recently elected to the City Council in Englewood, New Jersey, where I reside. After spending nearly four years as a Special Assistant U.S. Attorney with the U.S. Attorney's office in Brooklyn (where I represented the Immigration and Naturalization

Service among other federal agencies), I joined my father's firm—Wildes & Weinberg, which has exclusively practiced in the field of U.S. Immigration, Consular and Nationality Law for the past forty (40) years. We receive referrals and represent some of the finest individuals and most prominent companies in the world—as they settle themselves and their personnel in our country.

Over the last several years, I have also been retained by several high-profile individuals and whistle-blowers who have sought asylum in the United States. Chief among them are a Saudi Arabian diplomat (Mohammed Al-Khilewi) who defected after walking off with incriminating evidence of international terrorism and espionage; an accused terrorist (Hani Al-Sayegh) allegedly implicated in the Khobar Towers bombing in Saudi Arabia—an atrocity in which 19 U.S. servicemen lost their lives; and most recently a Pakistani nuclear scientist (Dr. Iftikhar Khan) who sought refuge on our shores with alarming information concerning nuclear proliferation and the transfer of nuclear weaponry between Pakistan, China and Iran. I considered it a privilege to represent my government at the U.S. Attorney's office—and have in each of the cases described above—been able to not only protect my client's interests but, in turn, these individuals have assisted U.S. law enforcement, furnishing useful information to combat terrorism and curtail nuclear proliferation (without violating the attorney-client privilege).

Current Need for Legislation

The rise in international terrorism against the United States, reflected in the recent bombings of U.S. embassies in Africa, highlights the need to provide the U.S. government with the tools to effectively protect U.S. security, prosecute terrorists, and send out a message that will deter further attacks and terrorist activity.

The State Department released a report last month indicating that there were 273 international terrorist attacks during 1998, a marked drop from the 304 attacks reported in 1997. While the total number of persons killed or wounded in terrorist attacks was the highest yet (741 dead and 5,952 individuals who suffered injury)—no acts of international terrorism occurred in the U.S. The decrease in international terrorism was attributed to increasing success in diplomacy, sophisticated counterterrorism initiatives, improved political conditions in troubled states, and greater law enforcement, which has successfully dismantled terrorist organizations.

Since the time of the founding fathers, Congress has enacted legislation to protect America from aliens who pose a security threat, beginning with the Alien and Sedition Laws of 1798. These laws authorized the President to deport "alien enemies"—resident aliens whose countries of citizenship were at war with the United States—and other aliens commonly referred to as "alien friends" whom the President judged to be dangerous to the peace and safety of the United States.

The Department of State has designated seven (7) countries as "State sponsors of terrorism" [Cuba, Iran, Iraq, Libya, North Korea, Sudan, and Syria], and acknowledged that many terrorist organizations still operate there independently, are highly mobile, and possess sophisticated technology. Dale Watson, Chief of the International Terrorism Section of the FBI, testified before the Senate Judiciary Committee on February 24, 1998, indicating that terrorists regularly employ the Internet and have a growing organizational presence in the United States requiring a stronger investigative and prosecutorial response. He added that significant numbers of Iranian students (419 in 1997) are admitted yearly to U.S. institutions—many of whom provide ongoing intelligence and technical expertise to the government of Iran.

Current Law Enforcement/INS Tools

Reflecting the growing awareness that numerous terrorist organizations operate and raise millions of dollars in the U.S. each year through ostensibly legitimate front organizations, in 1996 Congress passed the Antiterrorism and Effective Death Penalty Act (hereinafter "AEDPA"), which, along with numerous other tools for combating terrorism, provides for a special court for deporting alien terrorists. The main purpose of the special removal court is to streamline the process of deportation when the mere presence of a suspected alien terrorist in the U.S. is considered dangerous and disclosure of sensitive information and sources under normal immigration procedures would pose a risk to U.S. national security.

Since its enactment, the AEDPA has allowed for the deportation of immigrants based on secret evidence and imposes criminal and immigration sanctions against anyone who provides support, even humanitarian aid, to a foreign group labeled by the U.S. State Department as "terrorist." While the AEDPA is a significant legal tool and deterrent—it will take time for it to work.

The use of confidential information against aliens concerning national security matters has also been approved by the United States Supreme Court, and authorized by regulation or statute since the 1950s. Congress has expressly approved the use of classified information in recent statutes, and several Department of Justice regulations allow the Immigration and Naturalization Service (INS) to present relevant classified information, or secret evidence, in deportation proceedings.

Congressman Andrews' Proposed Legislation

Congressman Andrews' proposals are aimed at targeting those who "knowingly aided and abetted" an individual engaged in terrorist activity. It is well known that many radical organizations have established fictitious nonprofit institutions through which monies have then been channeled to purchase weapons and fund terrorist operations.

Terrorists must not be allowed to hide under the cloak of legitimate organizations or be able to avail their resources to facilitate terrorist activities. My own experience, having represented an alleged terrorist, gave me firsthand experience in dealing with matters involving our national security. These individuals know what buttons to push in order to come to our country. Once they land on our shores, many are able to bootstrap themselves onto safe legal ground and protect themselves in ways Congress never intended or could imagine. Ostensibly people can enter the United States on various visas and escape scrutiny.

Terrorists may now have settled anywhere in our country. Many terrorist organizations have, in fact, created smaller cells of operations and have associates who collaborate with one another in order to provide refuge and, in fact, share their resources. Some foreign dignitaries and diplomats stationed in the New York and Washington, DC area support terrorists, have provided diplomatic cover to known terrorists, and might themselves be considered "associates of terrorists." In another matter, we learned of diplomats who were able to smuggle in weapons and make-shift bombs, through their diplomatic pouches. This provision would provide a legal nexus to curtail these activities.

Moreover, Congress has promulgated similar measures in the past. In another case, a pro-bono matter in which I represent Patricia Roush—a woman whose children were kidnapped by her husband and taken to Saudi Arabia (after she was given full custody by American Courts)—we were successful through the efforts of Senator Feinstein in passing H.R. 4328 (passed 10/9/98) in amending the Immigration and Nationality Act rendering aliens inadmissible to the United States if they support an international child abductor, provide him or her with material support or safe haven, etc.

Constitutional Issues

The Courts will continue to delineate (through case law) their standards of "reasonable suspicion." Provided law enforcement is required to prove to a Court an actual nexus between the alien's conduct and the knowing aiding and abetting of terrorist activity—I believe the provision will withstand judicial/constitutional review. Moreover, Congress has provided a number of procedural safeguards in order to assure due process for the alien, such as the right to counsel, the right to present evidence, the right to confront witnesses, the right to receive a summary of classified evidence, and the right to appeal orders of removal.

Civil libertarians, in their efforts to declassify source information, have claimed that alien terrorist removal court proceedings are sufficiently similar to criminal trial proceedings and feel that the aliens should receive similar due process procedural safeguards. Other civil liberties groups are calling for the government to prove its case against the suspected alien terrorist by "clear and convincing evidence"—a much higher standard of proof. However, since deportation is legally considered by the Courts to be a much lesser deprivation of liberty than incarceration, and historically has been considered civil rather than criminal, in nature—the same level of procedural safeguards might not be constitutionally required. This is consistent with Congress' historic plenary power vis-à-vis aliens and the Supreme Court's concept of a sliding scale of rights wherein citizens are afforded more privileges than aliens.

The government clearly has an interest in prosecuting associates who aid and abet terrorists, maintaining the secrecy of highly sensitive intelligence, protecting the identity of its sources and avoiding compromising ongoing investigations. One can foresee situations in which alien terrorists or their associates could obtain classified information detailing what the U.S. knows about their organizations simply by purposely inviting deportation proceedings by the special removal court.

Critics have also claimed that these matters have singled-out Muslims. The overwhelming majority of Muslim immigrants to the U.S. are law abiding, and the critics should be assured that the INS and the U.S. government have no policy of singling-out Muslims for deportation. In fact, the great majority of those deported by the INS are not Muslims. Although the 25 aliens against whom classified evidence is being used in deportation proceedings are Muslims, this simply reflects that the most active global terrorist organizations against the United States in recent years have been militant Muslim organizations, such as Hamas, Islamic Jihad, and groups supported by billionaire terrorist Osama bin Laden.

Conclusion

Although terrorists act with a blatant disregard for life, we, as Americans, must continue to distinguish ourselves as a moral compass for the world community, and in our removal of these vicious individuals and their associates, still temper our actions with democracy and due process.

I believe that Congressman Andrews' proposal, the current alien terrorist removal court statute and other statutes allowing the use of classified information against suspected alien terrorists—reflect an adequate balance between our interest in preserving an individual's due process rights and our need to protect our national security. Since the bombing of the World Trade Center, we have developed a greater appreciation for the increasing magnitude of terrorist groups, and their insidious methods of operation. We must now protect our citizens from those who would aid and abet their activities and movements. I am confident that the Courts will strike the proper balance in construing these laws, and am grateful that we have these provisions of law—these weapons—to help combat terrorism.

Appendix B

An Oral Presentation Regarding Child Abduction

Background

I was recently elected to the City Council in Englewood, New Jersey, where I reside. After spending nearly four years as a Special Assistant U.S. Attorney with the U.S. Attorney's office in Brooklyn—where I represented the Immigration and Naturalization Service among other federal agencies—I joined my father's firm, Wildes & Weinberg, which has exclusively practiced in the field of U.S. Immigration, Consular and Nationality Law for the past forty (40) years. Working as a Federal Prosecutor was invaluable in exposing me to the resources and limitations of U.S. law enforcement with regard to international prosecutions and immigration controls. Our firm receives referrals and represents some of the finest individuals and most prominent companies in the world as they settle themselves and their personnel in our country.

Over the last several years, I have also been retained by several high-profile individuals and whistle-bowers who have sought asylum in the United States. Chief among them are a Saudi Arabian diplomat (Mohammed Al-Khilewi) who defected after walking off with incriminating evidence of international terrorism and espionage; an accused terrorist (Hani Al-Sayegh) allegedly implicated in the Khobar Towers bombing in Saudi Arabia—a tragedy in which nineteen U.S. servicemen lost their lives; and most recently a Pakistani nuclear scientist (Dr. Iftikhar Khan) who sought refuge on our shores with alarming information regarding nuclear proliferation and the transfer of nuclear weaponry between Pakistan, China, and Iran. I considered it a privilege to represent my government in the U.S. Attorney's office—and have in each of the case described above—been able not only to protect my client's interest—but in turn these individuals have assisted U.S. law enforcement, furnishing useful information to combat terrorism and curtail nuclear proliferation.

I suppose it was my federal law enforcement background that best prepared me to represent the prominent diplomats, scientists, and other international whistle-blowers who found their way to our shores and were willing to provide useful intelligence information in exchange for safe passage and refuge.

Introduction

With the increase of international travel as well as the greater numbers of marriages between nationals of different countries and United States citizens, international child abductions are on the rise. My presentation today is based on my experiences representing several clients over the course of the past few years as well as written materials that have been previously authored in the field. Since the 1970s the State Department has received 11,000 reports of American children being abducted to foreign countries. The number is always on the rise. Unfortunately, the annual number of children abducted from the United States has risen dramatically since—and these are only the *reported* cases.

While representing a Saudi diplomat in 1994, I had the privilege of first meeting Pat Roush—who just spoke—who introduced herself to me, advocating that her circumstances would further expose Saudi corruption and that her plight could benefit from my involvement. Since then, Pat and I have taken her cause to the highest levels of our government, we have marched ourselves through the halls of Congress—making law, noise, and impassioning others to fill the large gaps in our laws. I have represented Pat Roush since 1994 without a fee and many others since then on a "pro bono" basis. My heart goes out to these dear parents for the misery that they have endured, and find it personally rewarding to see to it that these laws are ultimately changed.

I am sure that our founding fathers would be quite disappointed that our government could broker tremendous financial arrangements with nations—even friendly nations—and negotiate the placement of military installations in very sensitive regions, but when it comes to negotiating the return of our young citizens kidnapped and taken abroad or when it comes to reconciling family disputes internationally—our government turns its back on its own citizens.

I have been asked to consult to major network television with regard to the Elián González matter of late, where many of these concerns have been raised. Whether you feel he was improperly abducted by his mother and should be returned to his father in Cuba or you believe that he deserves to remain in the United States—most would argue that we could all benefit from the exposure and precedent that will hopefully be culled out from this international escapade. In short, I can venture to say that no one in the room wants to see a young boy separated from his parent. Yet, I believe that the Attorney General did *not* treat this case appropriately. She could have averted the use of force had she originally entertained the applications put forward—when the young boy's father was not on United States soil.

More importantly, the fact that there was no settled law to ameliorate this dispute shows me that we have a lot of ground to cover. The precedent established in this case will have reverberations for many in the years to come. This case should have been off of the streets where politics on both sides played heavily into our system and distorted the issues at an earlier stage. What I find most intolerable is that the U.S. government has spent so much time and our tax resources when over 11,000 of our citizens have been ignored. The government has clearly taken advantage of the confusing legal arguments and the several venues involved in this matter. The most that we can expect from our State Department in over 11,000 other cases, however, is a list of attorneys, a welfare visit, and a sympathetic ear. Even the Justice Department fails to file international warrants in many case, labeling these parental abduction matters as "domestic-custody disputes." This is not acceptable when we pride ourselves on being the moral compass of the world. Parents who spirit their children away to foreign territories are no different from any other kidnapper and are in fact criminals. The photos of the young boy being returned to his father at the muzzle of a gun speaks very loudly that legislation and support is badly needed in this arena. Is this how we expect our children to be treated overseas when we want our children returned? Is the State Department and Justice Department condoning the use of force?

The State Department has adopted a policy of neutrality rather than advocating for the recovery of our children. Our young citizens ought to be able to enter our embassies abroad, secure their passports and the protection of our government, which should take strong diplomatic positions on such issues so that these children might return to our shores. I can think of no greater purpose for our embassies overseas to serve. How many children would still be with their parents had we instituted such concerned measures? Congress needs to enact statutes that would sanction governments that permit kidnapping, vigilantly prosecute kidnappers, and send a strong message to the governments of the world—so as to avert years of devastation caused by the many state, federal, and international loopholes in the law that enable child-kidnapping to prevail.

Just last week I was able to assist in the return of two young children kidnapped to France—where a family court in New York nearly refused to accept jurisdiction because the attorney and law secretary to the judge did not have a firm understanding of U.S. immigration law. Often there is a complex confluence of immigration, international, family, and state law and practice that needs to be mastered by attorneys representing their clients.

I am not an expert on Hague Convention law, nor am I a specialist in the family court process—I felt it appropriate in view of the many experiences that I've had to separate my presentation so as to provide more practical guidance to those who have either found themselves in circumstances where their children have been abducted and to those here who feel that they are at risk or can help those at risk.

Prevention of Abductions

Simply put, if you or a loved one are in a cross-cultural marriage—you need to evaluate your vulnerability and try to determine if you are indeed at risk. I have even found the "rooting" of an individual's intentions to eventually abduct a child can arise even in family vacations abroad or in the celebration of international holidays. These trips need to be carefully watched. I would suggest that couples secure as many names, addresses, contacts, and data that they can get their hands on. This includes the recording of passports, bank accounts, driver's licenses, and any old utility bills that you can get your hands on. The more writings you have—the more leads you might succeed in following in the future.

I have suggested taking many photos and fingerprints of your children on a regular basis—even along on your person when you travel so that you are prepared for all eventualities. I know parents who teach the children how to call collect and create all kinds of plans in the event of an emergent circumstance. Finally, if you feel that you are at risk, it is very important that you enlist a good attorney at an early stage so that you can evaluate your strongest legal options and plan accordingly. Often clients as well as members of their family require emotional support. I would suggest the enlisting of a good therapist as well. You need your wits about you. You need to garner as much emotional and financial support as you can from your loved ones and friends so that you are prepared to meet all the challenges that you may face.

Just because a couple has problems does not necessarily mean they need to go to war over the children. With today's society, as mobile as it is—separation agreements could be flexible and international child abductions could be averted with some creativity. I have heard from scores of parents that have prevented abductions by simply negotiating terms and leveraging what they can—both informally or in the courts.

Of course, if you feel you are at a total imminent risk—bodyguards should be hired and a 100 percent, 24-hour effort should be put into securing all legal rights and personal protection of the child—for both the child's protection and yours.

Once you've determined that you are vulnerable, and that your marriage is at an impasse—I would recommend your securing a decree of sole custody including an order preventing any travel abroad. Some courts will require a bond to be posted as a deterrent and these measures could be provided in separation agreements as well.

You should secure several certified copies of these documents so that you can provide them to schools and other custodial guardians. Certainly, you should alert the U.S. State Department Passport Division—to stop the issuance of a United States passport. Foreign embassies in the United States and embassies abroad should be alerted as well.

If a child is abducted, the first priority is to determine the exact location of the child and to secure an automatic freeze order and warrants from your state and Federal Courts. Whether you call your local police authority, the FBI, or any other law enforcement contacts you have—what is critical is a complete written summary of the actual circumstances perpetrated during the course of the abduction so that this information could be used by both police authority investigators and later in the legal system.

Letters and reports should be filed immediately with the National Crime Information Center as well as the State Department Children's Issues Desk—which will immediately alert their passport name check system. If you know where the child is—you should request a "welfare visit and whereabouts visit" from the local United States Embassy or Consulate as well.

I would suggest contacting relatives and friends both in the United States and abroad to enlist local civic support—your social center, church or synagogue, etc. You will need to prepare literature, posters, postal traces, and Department of Health locators as well as social security tracers.

Some parents have sought judicial subpoenas and search warrants in order to secure credit card information, old phone bills and other mechanisms by which you can locate a child's abductor. Even the E Z Pass—the little gizmo you use in order to go through a toll without paying—could provide information on the whereabouts of a child abductor. It is just as important to put out photos of the abducting parent as much as the children that have been abducted—which would be more readily recognizable to others who could assist you. Even if you feel that the parent has not yet left the U.S., I would suggest consulting with a foreign attorney and hiring yourself an attorney in the United States who is both familiar with immigration controls and family law. Be mindful that individuals with dual nationality may be traced through their passport requests. I would hesitate to cancel requests made of foreign passport authorities by abducting parents. You might find your former spouse and child in a third country by virtue of a passport application being filed at that site. Of course, you will also need to explore whether or not the country that you believe your child will be taken to ultimately supports extradition to the United States or not.

The more information you have at your disposal, the more data that you control—the greater the odds are that you will be able to react appropriately and secure your child. Due in great measure to Pat and my lobbying—immediate family members of those who aid and abet child abductors will now be prohibited from securing admission to the United States. We hope one day they too will also be prosecuted. It is so important for everyone to realize that not only will you be prosecuted if you kidnap a child—but if you provide a safe haven for an abductor—you will be sought out as well. Finally, if you are successful in securing the return of your children, you may nonetheless contemplate a full prosecution despite your initial success. There are federal statutes which mandate a three-year federal term of imprisonment for those who abduct children.

Depending upon the U.S. Attorney's office and the particular district, we have seen the government commence these criminal prosecutions. These are new statutes that need to be enforced, and encouraged. (Dr. Petrov-Syria matter.) Often the process of trying to secure your children back involves tremendous energy and time. I would recommend leaving no stone unturned, going on record in writing to every official with whom you have spoken, and calling other parents who have gone through this as well.

Hague Convention Cases

There is obviously a big difference if your child is abducted and taken to a country that has signed the Hague Convention. The Hague Convention sought to compel the return of a child to the child's state of habitual residence, in order to facilitate a proper determination of custody based on the child's "best interests." It is a procedural device for the return of a child—not a custody determination. Only fifty-three countries have ratified the Hague Convention. The language of the exceptions to the Hague Convention delegates significant discretion in ordering the return of an abducted child. Particularly, the "grave risk of harm" exception and the "consent" exception. A judge can refuse to return a child, if he or she finds that the child objects to being returned or has attained an age and degree of maturity at which it is appropriate to take account of the child's views. The court also has a broad degree of discretion in determining whether or not there is a "grave risk" in returning an abducted child to its home country and the Convention does not provide many threshold levels or standards.

For the past years I have been primarily dealing with countries that have not ratified the Hague Convention. I felt it appropriate to focus on the immigration controls and tools that could be useful. Since so few nations have become contracting states, many "safe harbors" have been created, greatly limiting the efficacy of the Hague Convention. A parent can now abduct a child and take it to a nonmember country with little immigration control: to date, we in the United States have no departure control system. What we do have depends totally on a person voluntarily presenting his or her own documentation to an airline.

The State Department reports that most child abductions reported since the 1970s have in fact been to noncontracting states. In addition, since the Hague Convention is not retroactive, it will also not affect children already abducted to a new signatory country. Thus, outstanding abduction cases cannot be resolved under this treaty. Statistics have indicated that the deterrence effect of the Hague Convention only applies to member nations as well.

To date, no Middle Eastern nation, with the sole exception of Israel, has signed on to become a member state. Many Southeast Asian countries are also not contracting states as well as are many Central and South American countries. Parents often abduct their children to a country in which they hold dual citizenship, or to which they have ethnic, cultural, or religious ties. Intercultural marriages have increased recently. The Middle East and Asia are perhaps the two most likely regions, and Muslim and Asian parents are especially motivated by religion and culture to abduct their children back to their native country. The Hague Convention cannot aid in the return of these children. In fact, the State Department released its human rights report, which fails to cite even one country for violating the Hague Convention on custodial parental rights.

What Do You Do If Your Child Is Taken to a Country That Doesn't Ratify the Hague?

In the absence of the Hague Convention, the domestic laws of the country in which the abducted child is located dictate custody. Islamic countries, for example, traditionally grant custody to the father. Rarely is an American woman granted custody of a child, regardless of whether she had converted to Islam. Saudi Arabian law, for example, even provides that, when the father is deceased, custody is granted to the closest living Saudi male relative, rather than to the American mother. This male bias is often relevant to abductions in the Middle East because most abductions are committed by the father.

Practice has shown that foreign courts give greater weight to the custody requests of their own nationals and that they are rarely resolved through diplomatic channels. Diplomatic ineffectiveness, coupled with Islamic cultural differences and bias, highly disadvantages American parents. Since a parent can abduct and retain a child with relative ease in a noncontracting state—I recommend going through the legal process overseas with competent counsel. First, you never know whether or not a particular country will use your case to make law, and what political events or buttons are being pushed at a particular time—rendering your case politically significant. Often deals are struck behind the scenes so as to quell adverse publicity.

Without the benefit of the Hague Convention, an aggrieved parent may ultimately have to litigate custody in the respective foreign court. If the litigation is unsuccessful and if diplomatic attempts to resolve the issue prove ineffective, no legitimate outlet remains. In desperate situations, coupled with love for a child, recovery attempts have been rampant. The United States State Department does not recommend the use of covert recoveries. It could violate the criminal law of the country in which it is attempted, and you could be prosecuted. A country has jurisdiction over a criminal act that has occurred within its territory, and sanctions vary from country to country.

Nonetheless, many American parents have employed mercenaries or private investigators, which have proven to be most expensive and effective. A parent might still be viewed as an accomplice or co-conspirator but usually escapes arrest by refraining from travel to that foreign country. It is interesting to note that most successful covert recoveries within the last decade have been from Hague signatory countries (Mexico, Germany, etc.)—serving as further evidence of the world's noncompliance.

The Hague Convention will not pose an obstacle to the successful recovery of a child. A parent who originally abducts a child will not be able to invoke Hague Convention protections.

The United States government will not honor a foreign decree obtained as a result of a "wrongful abduction" and thankfully will not encourage the taking of children from this country in order to obtain a more favorable custody determination in one's native country. If you engage in a covert recovery—you have to still be careful of perceptions, possible harm to the child during the extraction, and potential arrests. Of course, this is the extreme example as to why we require legislation and why significant congressional action is so vitally required.

What More Can We Do

Since the exceptions to the Hague Convention are problematic, safe harbors allow an abducting parent to escape, regaining custody through foreign courts is often futile, and recovery can be quite expensive—many believe that there is still more that can be done. These suggestions were made in writings I have seen through the years. I would refer you to a 1995 *Emory International Law Review* article by Tom Harper, who suggested that:

1. The global community must entice more countries to become parties to the Hague Convention, increasing its efficacy.

2. Legislatures should pursue other preventative measures to help deter abductions in the first place. There are actions that both parents and countries can take to reduce the risk of international abduction.

3. Parents who are involved in bi-cultural marriages should act preemptively to avoid an international abduction. Each could be required to put a large sum of money, post a bond, which would be forfeited in the event of an abduction. This would have two effects: First, it would deter a parent from abducting a child, as abduction would impose a direct substantial pecuniary loss on that parent. Second, the money can assist the aggrieved parent in securing the return of the child by defraying some of the expense in locating the child, litigation, custody or possible reabduction.

4. Governments can implement programs to help stop international abductions before they occur, including the training of customs officers to recognize high-risk situations. Other countries train their customs personnel to look for passengers who are nervous, or those who have excessive luggage for a short passage, derogatory comments made by a possible abductor, etc. Additionally, immigration and customs inspectors could be provided with hand-held computers that would display pictures and descriptions of missing children or international child abductors.

5. A national registry could be established that would register children at risk including those who are the subject of current custody litigation or who are otherwise perceived as high risk for child abduction. Immigration and Custom Agents could then cross-reference this registry along with their passport and airline controls in order to stop any international travel and hold potential abductors.

6. Bilateral treaties must be set up between countries that have not signed the Hague Convention. Simply put, if we can negotiate and conduct enormous business and commercial transactions with one

another—treaties could be ratified between nations to set up arbitration boards or tribunals to hear the merits of these matters. They could be comprised of representatives from both countries and may combine both American and foreign law. The cultural views of both the United States and the foreign country could find some common ground, even if it meant altering or removing certain provisions of the Hague Convention to suit their interests.

Conclusion

I currently represent several parents whose children have been kidnapped and taken to other countries. I have some success with Syria where we were able to retrieve three children several months ago and most recently—France. I am currently working with a client whose husband absconded with their child and returned to Lebanon. I am impassioned on behalf of my clients and find it unconscionable that our government has not better represented the interests of parents. The laws that we have on the books need to be vigilantly pursued, and our government must be encouraged to not only prosecute kidnappers to the fullest extent of the law—but must promulgate laws to fill the legal gaps. As the moral compass of the world, we need to send out a very strong message to those who would spirit our children away. Each time I am a guest on a network television show I receive scores of telephone calls from parents in similar circumstances. Our citizens need to be warned and educated so as to act preemptively rather than react in what can only be a devastating ordeal. I salute all of you in this room who have taken up this cause and am proud to stand among your ranks.

Appendix C

Immigration: The Nuts and Bolts

*The following pages offer a glimpse into the machinery for open-*ing the Golden Door, listing the various visa categories that people can use to enter the country, discussing permanent residency (that coveted green cared), and various responsibilities permanent residents might face.

Nonimmigrant Visa Categories

A nonimmigrant visa is a temporary visa. It is generally issued to people whose domicile is abroad who seek to be in the United States on a temporary basis.

The Nonimmigrant Visa Process

Nonimmigrant visas with alphabetical designations from A through V are issued by Foreign Service Offices of the U.S. Department of State at U.S. embassies and consulates abroad. Visas are stamped into a valid travel document, usually a passport. The visa bears the date of its issuance as well as the date of its expiration. It also designates the number of applications for admission at the U.S. border for which it is valid. A visa is only an entry document; it does not define visa status or length of stay permitted once a person is admitted to the United States.

At the border, the U.S. Department of Homeland Security (DHS), through its Customs & Border Patrol (CBP) division, has jurisdiction to admit the alien in the status for which the visa has been granted, and does so by recording the date of entry, the status in which the alien is admitted, and the duration of his or her authorized stay. (A record of admission may be printed from the CBP website.) Future extensions of stay or changes of nonimmigrant visa status are noted on a Form I-797 Notice of Approval, granted by another division of Homeland Security, now called Citizenship and Immigration Services (CIS), in response to an affirmative filing.

Citizens of Canada may present themselves at the border with appropriate documentation to request admission under the various nonimmigrant visa categories without first obtaining a visa stamp at a U.S. embassy or consulate, except for E-1, E-2 visas and K visas.

In addition, under a special program (the "Visa Waiver Program") nationals of thirty-eight countries to date have been allowed to enter the United States as visitors without first obtaining a visa stamp. *They must, however, first secure authorization to enter the United States online by utilizing the government's Electronic System for Travel Authorization ("ESTA") and are limited to a stay of a maximum of ninety days).*

Change from One Nonimmigrant Visa Classification to Another

An alien who enters in one nonimmigrant classification may, with certain exceptions, apply to change to another nonimmigrant status while in the United States. The application must be made while the alien is in lawful status, that is, during the authorized period of stay and prior to any violation of status such as unauthorized employment. Classifications that generally cannot be changed to another nonimmigrant classification in the United States are C, D, S, K, and visa waivers (J–1 in certain circumstances).

Change to Immigrant Classification
An immigrant visa is a permanent visa, synonymous with permanent resident or "green card."

An alien who enters in a nonimmigrant classification may, after the filing of a petition classifying the alien in a preference category, and usually after the approval of such a petition, apply to change status to that of a lawful permanent resident (evidenced by a green card) through a process called "adjustment of status." In cases where the alien otherwise qualifies for immigrant status, but has engaged in unauthorized employment while here temporarily, or has violated the terms of a nonimmigrant visa, immigrant status may, under certain circumstances, nevertheless be obtained through the issuance of an immigrant visa at an American Consular Post abroad. Any person seeking to adjust status from A, E, or G status must also file a waiver of immunities/special privileges.

Presumption of Immigrant Intent
By law, all persons applying for visas or for admission at the border as nonimmigrants are presumed to have the intention of residing here permanently as immigrants. (An exception to this rule applies to H and L visa holders and in some instances O-1 visa holders.) Accordingly, all intending nonimmigrants have the burden of proving that their intent is nonimmigrant in nature. For example, they must generally prove the existence of an unrelinquished foreign domicile to which they intend to return upon the conclusion of their temporary purpose in the United States. The same burden applies when applications are filed for extensions of nonimmigrant status, revalidation of nonimmigrant visas, or other benefits that presuppose an intention to depart.

Unlawful Presence
Overstaying past a period of authorized stay, even for one day, will invalidate the alien's nonimmigrant visa, which may not then be used for return to the United States. Moreover, with certain exceptions, an indi-

vidual who has overstayed by even one day may only apply for a new visa in the country of his or her *nationality*, eliminating "third country processing" at American consulates at more convenient locations (such as Canada or Mexico).

Other ramifications of unlawful presence render certain long-term overstays inadmissible to the United States. Any overstay of 180 days or more may have irreversible consequences. In view of these rules, it has become increasingly important to carefully monitor the status of individual nonimmigrants to ensure that no overstay occurs.

Nonimmigrant Classifications

A, Diplomats and Foreign Government Officials

An ambassador, public minister, diplomat or consular officer, cultural attaché or trade representative, or other foreign government official or employee, as well as their spouses and children, may be admitted as A-1 or A-2 nonimmigrants, and their attendants, servants, and personal employees and members of their families may be admitted as A-3 nonimmigrants, on the basis of reciprocity. Certain A-1 and A-2 dependents may be granted employment authorization. If an A visa holder seeks to adjust status to permanent residence, an application for a waiver of special privileges must be filed and can be submitted concurrently with the Adjustment of Status application.

B-1, Visitors for Business

A visitor for business is an alien who intends to conduct business in the United States that benefits a foreign employer, not in the nature of employment. He or she may not engage in local employment, nor displace a resident American worker, nor receive any direct remuneration for services from a United States source. Proper B-1 activities include, but are not limited to, meetings, audits, interviews, and inventory. The B-1 visitor may be initially admitted to the United States for a maximum period of one year until the purpose of the trip has been completed, and may apply for extensions of stay that are necessary to complete that purpose. In practice, due to heightened security concerns, most visitors are admitted for six months or less.

B-2, Visitors for Pleasure

A visitor for pleasure is an alien admitted for a personal visit to friends or relatives, on holiday, or for tourism. The initial period of admission is typically six months, allowing for a maximum stay of one year. Extensions of stay are permitted in appropriate circumstances. Persons coming primarily for the purpose of performing skilled or unskilled labor, study, or representing information media are not properly classifiable as B-2 visitors. Visitors may not attend school or engage in employment in the United States.

Visitors—Visa Waiver Program

Nationals visiting the U.S. from a list of certain countries, based on a historically low rate of nonimmigrant visa refusals, have been permitted to enter the United States as visitors for business or pleasure without first obtaining visas under the Visa Waiver Program. Individuals entering under this program are permitted to remain in the United States for a maximum period of ninety days and are barred from extending their stay or changing status while in the United States. These visitors are also prohibited from attending school or engaging in employment. DHS has now implemented an Electronic System for Travel Authorization (ESTA) that requires visa waiver applicants to receive an electronic travel authorization *prior to* departing for the United States. If ESTA clearance is denied, applicants must go to the U.S. consulate and obtain a B-1/B-2 visa even if they are a national of a waiver country. ESTA clearances are valid for two years.

C-1, Transit Aliens

A transit alien is an alien in immediate and continuous transit through the United States. A maximum period of twenty-nine days is authorized, not subject to extension or change of status.

D, Alien Crewmen

Alien crewmen, serving in such capacity while in port, are admitted for a maximum of twenty-nine days, not subject to extension. They may not work as crewmen except on the vessel or aircraft on which they arrived, or another similar vessel or aircraft of the same transportation company, and may not work on domestic flights. This nonimmigrant category is not subject to change of status to another nonimmigrant category.

E-1, Treaty Traders

A treaty trader is an alien who enters the United States in furtherance of the provisions of a Treaty of Commerce and Navigation between the United States and the foreign country of which the alien (and the alien's employer) is a national. For E visa purposes, a person is a national of a country whose passport he carries, regardless of place of birth, even though elsewhere in U.S. immigration law the concepts of nationality and citizenship are differentiated. The E-1 visa holder must be coming solely to carry on substantial trade principally between the United States and the foreign treaty country of which he or she is a national. The initial period of admission is for two years, although the visa may be granted for up to five years. Extensions of stay are possible upon filing an updated application reporting on the current volume of trade between the treaty country and the U.S. enterprise. There is no requirement for an overseas unrelinquished domicile, but the alien must intend to return to a home abroad once the purpose of admission has been accomplished. Treaty traders may apply for the E-1 visa at a U.S. embassy; the company does not need to file a petition to the immigration service. E-1 spouses are eligible for employment authorization.

E-2, Treaty Investors

An alien who enters pursuant to the provisions of a Treaty of Commerce and Navigation between the United States and the foreign country of which he or she is a national (same definition as for E-1, above), who is coming to the United States solely to develop and direct the operations of an enterprise in which the alien has invested, or is actively in the process of investing a substantial amount of capital, qualifies for E-2 status. The initial period of admission is two years, and the visa may be granted for up to five years, with extensions available in appropriate circumstances. Executives, managers, and essential specialized employees of foreign firms from a treaty country that have made a substantial investment may also qualify. Treaty investors may apply for the E-2 visa at a U.S. embassy; the company does not need to file a petition to the immigration service. E-2 spouses are eligible for employment authorization.

E-3, Professionals

An Australian national coming to perform services in a "professional specialty occupation" is eligible for the E-3 visa. This classification mirrors the standards of the H-1B visa category, described below: the job must be one that generally requires a related baccalaureate degree, the alien must have the appropriate credentials for the job, and the U.S. employer must file a labor condition application attesting that it will pay the prevailing wage for the job offered, and the benefits and working conditions offered to the E-3 professional will be similar to those offered to U.S. workers. However, an E-3 employer does not have to file a petition with U.S. Citizenship & Immigration Services. E-3 Australian professionals may apply for the E-3 visa at a U.S. embassy. Extension of stay and change of status can be filed in the United States; however, Premium Processing is not available for E-3 application. E-3 spouses are eligible for employment authorization. The period of admission is limited to two years but may be renewed or extended in certain circumstances. The E-3 professional must continue to demonstrate nonimmigrant intent. The annual cap of 10,500 E-3 visas has never been met.

F-1, Students (see also M-1 status for nonacademic students)

Bona fide students who seek to enter the United States temporarily and solely for the purpose of pursuing a full course of study in an educational program at an established institution of learning that has been approved by U.S. Citizenship & Immigration Services for attendance by foreign students can qualify for F-1 status. Prior to issuance of an F-1 visa or application for a change of status in the United States, the prospective student must be admitted by the school and issued an authorizing document, a Form I-20, approved by the Designated School Official, and the student must present this document in order to be accorded F-1 classification. F-1 visa status may not be accorded to an alien for the purpose of attending public elementary schools or publicly funded adult education programs. F-1 visas may only be accorded for attendance at public secondary schools after the alien reimburses the educational agency administering the school for the expense of providing such education and the proposed period of stay does not exceed twelve months. The alien spouse and minor children of such aliens are classified in F-2 category. F-2 spouses and children are not eligible for work authorization.

Schools and students are carefully monitored through an interactive database system known as SEVIS that tracks all U.S. schools that sponsor nonimmigrant students, and monitors the current status of all nonimmigrant students registered in the system, both before and after they are admitted to the United States.

Students are generally admitted for "duration of status." Duration of status is defined to include the program of study, any period of practical training authorized, plus an additional grace period of sixty days (if a student does not complete the course of study he or she is not entitled to the sixty-day grace period). Students must obtain permission in advance to accept employment. Authorization for part-time employment is issued in very limited circumstances (although not in the first year of the program), either based upon unforeseen financial hardship or for practical training relating to the course of study (known as curricular practical training or CPT). Students granted CPT may work up to twenty hour per week during school sessions or forty hours per week on vacations and school recesses. A period of optional practical training (OPT) may also be authorized for a period following the student's completion of a bona fide educational program. The amount of time spent in CPT can be deducted from the maximum amount of time permitted on OPT (one year). If a student completes one full year on CPT, the student will not be permitted to engage in OPT.

If a student does not work for ninety days consecutively during OPT, then OPT becomes invalid and the student must leave. OPT may only be granted once for each level of study. Thus, if a student completes a bachelor's degree and completes one year of OPT and then goes back to school and completes another bachelor's degree, he or she will not be eligible for a new period of OPT. However, if the student enrolls in a master's degree program and completes it, he or she will be eligible for another year in OPT.

Students currently engaged in postcompletion OPT who have completed a degree in a STEM (science, technology, engineering, or mathematics) field may apply for an additional seventeen months of employment authorization, for a total of twenty-nine months of employment authorization. Students must file an application with USCIS to apply for the STEM Extension. During the STEM Extension period, students may only work for employers who are enrolled in the E-Verify system, and the employer must agree to update immigration when the student leaves or the employment is terminated.

What Is the Cap-Gap Extension?

The USCIS now extends the authorized period of stay for all F-1 students who have filed an H-1B petition and change of status request (filed under the cap for the next fiscal year) prior to the expiration of their OPT employment authorization card. If USCIS approves the H-1B petition, the student is given an extension that enables him or her to remain in the United States until the requested start date indicated on the H-1B petition. The Designated School Official (DSO) at the Office of International Students(OIS) will process the Cap-Gap Extension I-20 on behalf of the student. In order for the DSO to indicate that a student has a Filed or Waitlisted Cap-Gap Extension, the student must be able to provide proof that the H-1B petition has been timely filed. If the H-1B petition is filed (and accepted) while the EAD is still valid, the student's work authorization is also extended until October 1st when the H-1B takes effect. If the H-1B is filed (and accepted) during the student sixty-day grace period, then the student is authorized to remain in the United States until the H-1B takes effect, but their work authorization is not extended through October 1st.

G, Employees of International Organizations

G visas are available to representatives, officers, and employees of certain international organizations that are not classifiable as U.S. employers, such as the United Nations, the World Bank, the World Health Organization, and so forth, as well as to their family members, servants, and personal employees. If a G visa holder seeks to adjust status to permanent residence, an application for a waiver of special privileges must be filed and can be submitted concurrently with the Adjustment of Status application.

H-1B, Specialty Occupation Workers

An alien coming temporarily to the United States to perform services in a "professional specialty occupation" qualifies for H-1B visa status upon approval of a petition filed by a sponsoring U.S. employer. By statute and precedent decision, qualified occupations are those that require at least a four-year baccalaureate degree related to the job (or its equivalent) as a prerequisite to entry-level employment. A qualified alien is a person who has the appropriate education and training for the offered position. An H-1B position is offered to the alien for a temporary period, but the position itself can be of an ongoing nature. H-1B aliens are admitted for the period of time requested by the employer in a petition to classify the alien in H-1B status, not to exceed an initial period of three years, and extensions of stay may be obtained in appropriate circumstances. The statute places a limit of six years on staying in H-1B status, but exceptions apply in certain circumstances when a U.S. employer has filed an immigrant visa petition or application for labor certification more than a year before the expiration of the H-1B worker's sixth year in H-1B status.

There is a numerical limitation on how many new H-1 approvals can be issued in any fiscal year (October 1 through September 30), which has lately resulted in H-1B visas being unavailable for much of the year. In addition, filing fees for this visa category are very substantial. Recent changes in the forms and interpretation have made it more difficult for an individual with an ownership interest in the petitioning organization to obtain H-1B status.

The Labor Condition Application (LCA)

As a prerequisite to filing a petition for an H-1B specialty occupation worker, the U.S. employer must file a labor condition application with the Department of Labor, attesting that the foreign professional will be paid at least the prevailing wage for the occupation. Included in this attestation, which provides the title and salary for the position and the location where the nonimmigrant will work, is an assertion that the actual wage level paid to other employees or the prevailing wage (whichever is higher) will be paid to the foreign H-1B professional, that the foreign worker's employment will not adversely affect the working conditions of similarly employed U.S. workers, that there is not a strike, lockout, or work stoppage involved in this employment, and that notice of the filing has been either provided to the bargaining representative or, if there is no bargaining representative, that such notice has been properly posted. Employers are required to retain the LCA with other documentation in a "Public Access File" which must be available for inspection for one year past the date of the LCA's expiration or one year from its withdrawal.

H-2, Temporary Workers

This category is available to aliens coming temporarily to perform services or labor that meet a temporary need, provided that unemployed people capable of performing such services cannot be found in the United States. Prearranged employment with a U.S. employer must exist, and the employer must first apply for a temporary labor certification, demonstrating to the U.S. Department of Labor that Americans capable of performing these services cannot be located and that the alien is coming to perform services that are themselves temporary in nature. A grant of certification by the U.S. Department of Labor shows U.S. Citizenship & Immigration Services that American workers are unavailable, and the petition may go forward. H-2A visas are available for temporary agricultural workers; H-2B visas are available for other temporary positions for which the U.S. employer can demonstrate a temporary need for workers that is seasonal, peak load, one-time, or serves an intermittent need. The initial period of admission may not exceed 364 days. Extensions may be obtained in very limited circumstances. H-2 visa status is limited to a maximum of three years.

Like the H-1B visa, there is a numerical limitation on how many new H-2 approvals can be issued in any fiscal year, which results in such visas being unavailable for significant parts of the year. The H-2 numerical quota is semi-annual and thus opens twice per year.

H-3, Trainees

A trainee is an alien coming temporarily to the United States for formal, structural training at the invitation of an individual, organization, firm, or other trainer in any field of endeavor, including agriculture, commerce, communications, finance, government, transportation, and the professions as well as in a purely industrial establishment. The petitioner must describe the type of training to be given, the source of remuneration of the trainee and whether or not any benefit will accrue to the petitioner, and must demonstrate why it is necessary for the alien to be trained in the United States, why such training is unavailable in the alien's home country abroad, and why the U.S. employer is willing to incur the cost of training. The trainee is not permitted to engage in productive employment unless it is incidental and necessary to the training and may not engage in employment that will displace a U.S. worker; the U.S. employer-trainer may not use H-3 trainees to fill positions ordinarily held by U.S. workers. The period of initial admission is that requested in a petition filed by the sponsoring employer-trainer and approved by USCIS, generally the full period required for training, but not to exceed two years.

I, Journalists and Foreign Media Representatives

An alien is admitted in I status, on a reciprocal basis, as a bona fide representative of a foreign press, radio, film, or other foreign information media organization, who seeks to enter the United States solely to engage in such vocation, and the spouse and children of such representative. A media representative must have press credentials and a signed contract of employment with the foreign media organization or its U.S. bureau, affiliate, or branch office. The initial period of admission is for the duration of the offered employment. An I visa will typically be issued for the full term of the employment contract, as limited by visa reciprocity rules. Admission in I visa status constitutes an agreement by the alien not to change media or to change employers without obtaining prior approval from the immigration service.

J, Exchange Visitors

An alien who is a bona fide student, scholar, trainee, teacher, professor, research assistant, specialist, or leader in a field of specialized knowledge or skill, coming temporarily as a participant in a program designated by the Department of State for the purpose of teaching, instructing, lecturing, studying, observing, conducting research, practical training, and so forth in an approved exchange program, and the alien's spouse and minor children of such participant, are admissible in J-2 visa categories. Certain J-1 aliens, and their dependents, are required by law to return to their own country for a period of two years to impart the knowledge they have gained in the United States before they may apply for H or L visas, or status as immigrants, unless a waiver of such two-year period is granted. The J exchange visitors subjected to this two-year foreign residency requirement include doctors who receive postgraduate medical training in the United States, trainees whose programs receive government funding, and any scholars or trainees whose exchange program is in a field designated by the home country as a skill set that country wishes to retain. The initial period of admission for a J nonimmigrant is as specified on the authorizing Form DS-2019 (formerly IAP-66) issued by the program sponsor, which varies according to the type of exchange program—up to three years for scholars, teachers, and research fellows; up to eighteen months for trainees.

The status of J-1 exchange visitors and their programs is carefully monitored through the Department of Homeland Security's interactive SEVIS database in much the same way as the status of F-1 students.

J-1 trainees must have completed a bachelor's degree abroad and have one year experience in the field or have five years experience in the field. Individuals who graduated from U.S. colleges and universities are NOT eligible for J-1 visa status unless they have another foreign degree or five-year experience on which the training is based. J-1 status may also be granted for an "internship" for a period of twelve months to a foreign national who completed a bachelor's degree abroad within the past twelve months.

K-1, Fiancé(e)s of U.S. Citizens

Those engaged to be married to U.S. citizens who seek to enter the United States solely to enter into a valid marriage with the U.S. citizen petitioner within ninety days after entry, and the minor children of such persons, may be admitted in K-1 and K-2 visa status. The period of admission is ninety days. K-1 aliens are ineligible for extension or change of nonimmigrant visa status; they may only adjust status to lawful permanent resident on the basis of marriage to the U.S. citizen petitioner.

K-3, Spouses of United States Citizen Petitioners

The K-3 visa classification is available to individuals who marry a United States citizen abroad and wish to enter the United States with their spouse and their minor child (K-4) to file and process an adjustment of status application.

L-1, Intracompany Transferees

An L-1 intracompany transferee is an individual who has been employed for one year of the past three years in a managerial or executive capacity by a foreign firm or corporation and seeks to enter the United States temporarily to continue to render his services to an affiliate or subsidiary thereof in a capacity that is also managerial, executive, or involves specialized knowledge not readily available in the U.S. job market. An L-1 petition filed with USCIS may be granted for an initial period of up to three years. Extensions may be available thereafter in increments of no more than two years, if such need is sufficiently documented. The statute limits the total stay in L-1 status (or L-1 and H-1 status combined) to five consecutive years for L-1B "specialized knowledge" visas and seven years for L-1A "executive" or "managerial" visas. The spouse and minor children (L-2) of such aliens are generally granted periods of admission and extension of stay to match those of the primary applicant, and L-2 spouses are eligible for employment authorization.

M-1, Nonacademic Students

Bona fide students seeking to enter the United States to pursue a full course of study at an established vocational or other recognized nonacademic institution, other than in a language training program, qualify for M-1 visas. The alien spouse and minor children of such aliens are classified in the M-2 category. Nonacademic students are admitted for the period of their school program plus thirty days. A very limited period of "practical training" may be authorized at the end of the program, which requires employment authorization.

N, Relatives of Employees of Certain
International Organizations

Certain relatives of long-term employees of the United Nations and other international organizations are eligible to remain in the United States under this provision.

O-1, Aliens of Extraordinary Ability

O-1 visas are issued to aliens of "extraordinary ability" in the sciences, education, business, and athletics who have demonstrated "sustained national or international acclaim and recognition for achievements in the field of expertise" showing that the alien "is one of the small percentage who have risen to the very top of the field." The standard for extraordinary ability in the arts is "distinction," as supported by evidence that the alien is "recognized as being prominent in the field." The standard for athletics, business, or science is "outstanding achievement." A petition must be filed with the immigration service, either by a U.S. employer, for ongoing employment, or by a U.S. agent for a defined series of engagements supported by a contract or contracts, and an itinerary stating where and when the alien of extraordinary ability performs services. Advisory consultation with a labor union, management organization, or other peer group is required. Short of a major, widely recognized international award, at least three types of evidence must be provided. The maximum period of initial admission permitted is three years, which may be renewed or extended in one-year increments thereafter, but there is no fixed limit on the total length of stay. O-1 visa status will only be granted for the amount of time necessary to fulfill the itinerary. The alien must show that he or she is sustaining the acclaim to be eligible for renewal of O-1 status.

O-2, Assistants to Aliens of Extraordinary Ability

O-2 visas are issued to aliens entering for the purpose of assisting the performance of an alien of extraordinary ability must establish that they are an integral part of the performance because of critical skills or long-standing relationship with the principal performing alien. An O-2 is not authorized to work independent of the O-1 principal alien and will be admitted for the same length of time as the principal.

P-1, Athletes and Entertainers

Athletes performing as individuals or teams and artists performing as part of an internationally recognized entertainment group are issued P-1 visas. The group must be based abroad, and at least 75 percent of the members must have been with the group for one year or more. A petition must be filed with the immigration service by a U.S. agent or employer, including a contract and itinerary stating where and when the group will perform or compete. Like the O-1, the P visa requires consultation with appropriate labor unions, or peer groups in occupations where there is no union. The maximum period of initial admission for an athlete is five years, for a team it is one year, and for an entertainment group, up to one year, if supported by contracts and itinerary. Support staff may enter with the entertainment group. They are granted P-1S classification. This requires a separate petition.

P-2, Athletes and Entertainers (Reciprocal Exchange)

Athletes and entertainers entering the United States to perform under reciprocal exchange programs are issued P-2 visas. This category is not petition based and generally does not require labor consultation because the reciprocal exchange is customarily between two unions, one in the United States and one abroad.

P-3, Athletes and Entertainers (Culturally Unique)

Athletes and entertainers entering to perform in a culturally unique program are issued P-3 visas. The individual or group must show some evidence of distinction in the art form or sport (examples include flamenco, Kabuki, capoeira). Like the P-1, a majority of the group must have worked together for at least a year, a petition must be filed with the immigration service by a U.S. agent or employer, including a contract and itinerary stating where and when the group will perform or compete, and a labor advisory opinion from a union or peer group is required. The maximum period of initial admission is three years, if supported by contracts and itinerary, and P-3 status may be extended for a maximum stay of five years.

Q, Cultural Exchange

Aliens entering the United States to participate in designated international cultural exchange programs that provide practical training, employment and sharing of culture may obtain Q visas. The maximum period permitted under this visa category is fifteen months.

R, Religious Workers

Certain religious workers entering the United States to perform work in a religious vocation, religious profession, or traditional religious occupation for a bona fide nonprofit religious organization in the United States, who have had membership in the same religious denomination as the sponsoring U.S. organization for at least two years preceding the application, and their spouses and children, qualify for R visas. Recent changes to the regulations now require that the U.S. sponsor first file a petition with USCIS before the visa application can be made. Additional recent strictures require an investigatory visit to the premises of the sponsoring organization prior to the granting of the petition. The initial period of approval has also been reduced from thirty-six months to thirty months; extensions for an additional thirty months may be obtained. Premium Processing is available for this visa category, but only if the organization has undergone a recent investigatory visit (i.e., has a recent approval).

S, Witnesses and Informants

Certain aliens who will be serving as witnesses in federal or state court with respect to criminal enterprises, when such alien is determined by the attorney general to possess critical and reliable information; certain aliens who will provide critical and reliable information, as determined by the secretary of state and attorney general jointly, respecting terrorist organizations or operations, to federal law enforcement authorities or a federal court, and where appropriate the spouse, married or unmarried sons and daughters and parents of such alien, may be accorded S visas. The S visa may not be changed to another nonimmigrant visa in the United States.

T, Certain Victims of Trafficking in Persons

Certain aliens who have been victims of severe forms of trafficking in persons who are physically present in the United States and have assisted in the investigation of the prosecution of acts of trafficking and the spouse, children, and parents of such victim maybe eligible for this classification.

TN, Entrants Under NAFTA

Citizens of Canada or Mexico who seek temporary entry as business persons to engage in certain designated business activities at a professional level may be admitted to the United States in accordance with the terms of the North American Free Trade Agreement (NAFTA). Such individuals are currently admitted with the TN visa designation for an initial admission of up to three years. TNs are not limited to the number of years they may be in TN status, but TN holders are subject to prove nonimmigrant intent.

U, Victims of Severe Criminal Activity/Materials Witnesses

Aliens who have suffered substantial physical or mental abuse as a result of having been a victim of criminal activity involving violation of one or more of certain federal, state, or local criminal statutes relating to rape, torture, trafficking, incest, domestic violence, and other such similar crimes and individuals having knowledge of such crimes may under appropriate circumstances be eligible for this visa classification.

V, Special Limited Provision for Spouses and Children of Permanent Residents

Aliens who could be classified in the V nonimmigrant category if the beneficiary of a petition according preference status was filed with the attorney general on or before December 21, 2000. Children of the principal alien are eligible to receive this benefit as well.

Permanent Resident (Immigrant) Alien Status Categories

The status of a lawful permanent resident of the United States may be obtained by applicants who meet both the qualitative and quantitative requirements of the law. Qualitatively, they must prove themselves not to be ineligible for immigrant status under any of the general categories of inadmissible aliens specified in the law (8 U.S.C. 1182(a)), including criminality, fraudulent use of documents, mental defect, Communist party affiliation, drug trafficking, terrorism, contagious diseases of public health significance, and so forth. Quantitatively, they must either obtain a family preference classification based on the petition of specified close relatives who are citizens or lawful permanent residents of the United States; or based on the petition of a sponsoring employer or prospective employer for an employment-based preference; or based on a major invest-ment in the United States; or through extraordinary ability; or through selection through the Diversity (lottery) Visa program. The effect of the law's national and worldwide quota limitations often results in extended waiting periods before permanent resident status may be finally obtained. Such status may be sought either through an immigrant visa application before a U.S. consular officer abroad or, in certain circumstances, in adjustment of status proceedings within the United States.

Employment-Based Immigrants

The Immigration Act of 1990 presented Congress's most recent revision of the visa allocation formula. The great majority of these visas are allo-cated for the various categories of family reunification, and140,000 visas are provided for employment-based immigration.

The Immigration Act now defines five categories or preferences (of which three have additional subcategories of their own) for immigration based on employment or employment-creation:

*Preference I: "Priority Workers" (40,000 Visa Numbers
Available Plus Spill Down from Preferences IV And V)
Employment I, Subcategory I (E11)
Aliens with "Extraordinary Ability" in Arts, Sciences,
Education, Business, or Athletics.*

To qualify in this subcategory, the applicant must show that he or she is one of that small percentage who have risen to the very top of their field of endeavor and must be able to demonstrate that his or her contribution would "substantially benefit" the United States prospectively.

This category does not require an employer to file the petition. It can be a "self-petition."

*Employment I, Subcategory II (E12)
Outstanding Professors and Researchers.*

To qualify in this category, the applicant must establish international recognition or acclaim and must show at least three years of full-time experience in teaching or research in the field, and must have an offer of full-time employment for a tenured or tenure-track teaching position, or a comparable research position in private industry in an organization that has a full-time research staff of three or more individuals. The petitioner itself must also be shown to have acclaim.

*Employment I, Subcategory III (E13)
Certain Multinational Executives and Managers.*

A person who was working abroad in a managerial or executive position for one year or more in the three-year period immediately prior to transfer into the United States, who has been offered a similar managerial or executive position in the United States with a parent, subsidiary, branch, or affiliate of the same company he or she worked for abroad, qualifies for this immigrant visa category, whether or not he or she has a university degree.

*Preference II: Professionals and Aliens of "Exceptional Ability"
(40,000 Visa Numbers Available Plus Spill Down
from Preference I)*

Immigrant status is available to qualified immigrants who are members of the professions holding advanced degrees or their equivalent, or who because of their exceptional ability (which must be demonstrated by more than just a degree or license) in the sciences, arts, or business, will substantially benefit prospectively the national economy, cultural, or educational interests, or welfare of the United States.

Normally certification must be obtained from the Department of Labor that there are not American workers ready, willing, and available for the position, in most cases (See "Labor Certification" below). However, such certification and a specific job offer may be waived for applicants in this category if their work is established to be in the national interest, and if the workers possess an advanced degree or have exceptional ability in their field of endeavor. However, a precedent case decided in 1998 substantially narrowed the National Interest Waiver category. Such cases must now meet three stringent tests: (1) the field of endeavor in which the alien works must have substantial intrinsic merit, (2) the benefits from the alien's work must be national in scope, and (3) the prospective benefits to the United States from the alien's prospective work must be great enough to outweigh the benefit inherent in protecting the U.S. labor market.

Also, aliens who have demonstrated exceptional ability in the sciences or arts (except the performing arts) may be eligible for another classification that avoids labor certification, called Schedule A, Group II, if they can show substantial extrinsic evidence of their achievements, similar to the "extraordinary ability" category described above.

Labor Certification—The PERM Process

The Department of Labor has a complex procedure for certifying that a job may be offered to a foreign worker because the employer has tested the labor market and found that there are no qualified U.S. workers available to fill the offered position. This is called permanent alien labor certification, or "PERM," an acronym for the electronic filing system, implemented in March 2005. The process includes a set of mandatory recruitment efforts by the employer to test the U.S. labor market, which must be completed within a specific time frame before an application can be filed and a certification can be issued by the Department of Labor.

A PERM filed under the second preference must entail a job offer for a position that requires a person to have a bachelor's degree plus five years experience or a master's degree as a minimum requirement before entering into that position and properly performing the job duties.

Preference III: Skilled Workers, Professionals and Other Workers (40,000 Visas Per Year Plus Any Unused Visas Under Preferences I and II)
Employment III, Subcategory I (E31)
Skilled Workers
An alien qualifies as a skilled worker if at the time of petitioning for classification the alien qualifies to perform skilled labor requiring at least two years' training or experience and is being sponsored for a position that is not temporary or seasonal in nature, for which qualified workers are not available in the United States. This category requires the use of the alien labor certification process.

Employment III, Subcategory II (E32) Professionals
This category is reserved for professionals, defined as aliens holding baccalaureate degrees and members of the professions employed in positions for which United States workers are not available. This category requires the use of the alien labor certification process.

Employment III, Subcategory III (EW)
"Other Workers"
This subcategory is reserved for aliens capable of performing unskilled labor not of a temporary or seasonal nature for which qualified workers are not available in the United States. Since a cap of 10,000 visas (within this overall 40,000 limit) is set for applicants seeking to qualify as "other workers," there is a substantial waiting period under this subcategory. This category requires the use of the alien labor certification process.

Schedule A, Group I: Precertified Shortage Occupations
Unlike all other occupational groups in the employment-based third preference category, two groups have been "precertified" by the labor department due to long-standing critical labor shortages throughout the United States: Registered Nurses and Physical Therapists. U.S. employers do not need to go through alien labor certification to sponsor workers in these two occupations. There were 50,000 visas allocated to this sub-

category. However, the 50,000 visas were exhausted several years ago so, regardless of the shortage, individuals in these two occupations face significant delays due to quota backlogs. Regardless of the visa allotment being unavailable, these occupations remain exempt from the filing of a labor certification with the Department of Labor (PERM) and all advertising requirements associated with that filing.

Preference IV: Special Immigrants (10,000 Visas Available Per Year)

This category is reserved for certain qualified special immigrants such as religious workers, victims of spousal abuse, certain former United Nations employees, and so forth. The religious worker special immigrant category is distinguished from the temporary religious worker visa by an important feature: it requires two years' prior full-time paid work experience in a religious occupation, profession, or the ministry, as opposed to merely two years' prior membership in the religious denomination of the sponsoring U.S. tax-exempt religious organization.

Preference V: Employment-Creation Immigrants (10,000 Visas Available Per Year)

This "investor" provision provides visas to applicants who invest a minimum of a million dollars in a new commercial enterprise in the United States that will result in the creation of employment for at least ten "qualified workers" (United States citizens and permanent residents) other than immediate family members of the investor. In certain exceptional circumstances, including when the investment is made in an area of high unemployment or a rural area, the amount may be reduced to $500,000. An investor may commit $500,000 to a preapproved Regional Center, in which case employment of ten U.S. workers may be "indirect" and attributable to the Regional Center's project. The permanent residence is granted for a two-year period. Within ninety days of its expiration, the applicant must file a petition to remove the conditions on his or her residency. This petition (form I-829) is adjudicated at the goal of ensuring that the investment is still at risk, that the investment vehicle is still engaged in the same business activities, and that the appropriate number of employees are still employed with the enterprise.

EB-5 statistics for fiscal year 2012 showed that I-526 immigrant petitions by alien entrepreneurs were being approved at a 79 percent clip and I-829 petitions by entrepreneurs to remove the conditions of residence status at a 92 percent rate. The number of approved I-526 petitions grew from 640 in 2008 to 3,700 in the last fiscal year.

Chinese nationals comprise a very large percentage of filing, and there is now a quota backlog for Chinese nationals.

Family-Sponsored Preferences and Diversity Immigrants

(a) Family Sponsored Immigrants

Immediate relatives of U.S. citizens (including the spouse, minor children, and parents of adult U.S. citizens) remain an unrestricted category, not subject to numerical limitation and therefore not subject to long waiting periods. However, the number of immediate relative applicants admitted is tabulated and can influence and reduce the number of visas available in the family-sponsored preference categories.

Family relationships also eligible for preference consideration are the following:

First Preference	Unmarried Sons and Daughters of United States Citizens
Second Preference	Divided into two Subcategories; Subcategory 2A: Spouses and Unmarried Children of Permanent Resident Aliens Subcategory 2B: Unmarried Adult Sons and Daughters of Permanent Resident Aliens
Third Preference	Married Sons and Daughters of United States Citizens
Fourth Preference	Brothers and Sisters of United States Citizens

(b) Diversity Immigrants

"Diversity immigration" is another of the euphemisms found in the Immigration Act of 1990. In fact, the Diversity Visa lottery program designates each year a list of countries that have comprised only a very small percentage of immigrants from immediately preceding years, and citizens of these countries may file an electronic application with the State Department for possible random or chronological selection for immigrant visas without any reference to the applicant's relationship to a United States sponsor. However, the application period is limited to one month per year (October), and under present regulations, a lottery applicant must have at least a high school education or two years' experience in a position that requires such experience.

Tax Notes

Who Is a Resident for Tax Purposes?

The Deficit Reduction Act of 1984 creates a statutory definition of the term "resident alien" for tax purposes. Included are two tests, one based on visa status and the other based on "substantial presence" in the United States.

Pursuant to I.R.C. Section 7701(b)(1)(A)(i), an alien who has been granted the immigration status of U.S. permanent residence is a resident for U.S. tax purposes, without exception. Absence from the United States for the entire year does not prevent the absolute determination that the person is a resident for tax purposes unless the status of permanent residence has been terminated under the immigration laws: I.R.C. Sec. 7701(b)(5). Permanent residence status can be relinquished in appropriate cases.

Under the "substantial presence" test, an individual is a resident for tax purposes if he has been physically present in the United States for 183 days or more within the calendar year: I.R.C. Sec. 7701(b)(3)(A)(ii). Alternatively, one is deemed "substantially present" in the United States if he has been "cumulatively present" in the United States over the last three years for a sufficient number of days. Cumulative presence is calculated by means of a complex formula set forth in the statute. An exception to the cumulative presence rules is provided for an individual alien who is able to show that his "tax home" and family connections remain in a foreign country. Teachers, students, and certain employees of foreign government agencies are generally exempt from the resident alien rules.

Important Rules Relating to Tax Avoidance

On August 21, 1996, the president signed into law the Health Insurance Portability and Accountability Act of 1996, which applies special tax rules to U.S. citizens who renounce their citizenship and certain green card holders who give up their resident status for the purpose of avoiding U.S. taxes.

A U.S. citizen who renounces citizenship for the purpose of avoiding federal income, estate, or gift taxes will be taxed as a citizen on both U.S. source income and any income "effectively connected" with a U.S. trade or business for ten years after expatriation. An individual will be presumed to have renounced citizenship to avoid taxes if his or her average annual net income for the five years preceding renunciation was greater than $100,000 or his or her net worth is $500,000 or more. Certain exceptions to the presumption apply.

Any "long-term resident" of the United States who ceases to be a lawful permanent resident or who commences to be treated as a tax resident of another country under a treaty tie-breaker provision will receive similar tax treatment. A "long-term resident" is a non-U.S. citizen who has been a lawful permanent resident of the United States in at least eight of the fifteen years preceding the loss of residence or assumption of tax residence in another country.

The foregoing is a brief summary only, and it is important to review the details carefully with tax counsel as they may apply to individual cases. The tax rules went into effect as of February 6, 1995.

In a related provision, under IIRAIRA, signed into law September 30, 1996, persons who officially renounce U.S. citizenship after the date of the act and are found by the attorney general to have done so for tax avoidance purposes *are inadmissible to the United States*. A determination will be made applying the IRS presumption and rules noted above. This provision applies only to former U.S. citizens, not to former lawful permanent residents. Waivers may be available for visiting the United States.

A Word About Estate Taxes and Immigration Status

Pursuant to IRC Section 2056(d), as amended in November 1988, in cases of transfers made by a U.S. citizen or resident decedent to a surviving spouse who is not a citizen of the United States, the marital deduction is not available unless there is a disposition by means of a qualified domestic trust. Accordingly, it may be important for foreign spouses to consider applying for naturalization to become U.S. citizens to avoid excessive estate taxes.

Note that the Health Insurance Portability and Accountability Act of 1996 also extended expatriate estate and gift tax provisions to certain long-term U.S. residents who terminate U.S. residency, and applied the presumption of tax avoidance noted above with respect to certain high-income or wealthy decedents.

Index

K

K-1 visas, 157–158
K-3 visas, 158
Karim, Rezai, 93–97
Kaufman, Irving, 4–5
KGB, 56, 64, 100–101
Khan, Abdul Qadeer, 78, 83–84
Khan, Ayub Gohar, 81
Khilewi, Mohammed al-, 33, 43–51, 56, 58, 61, 86, 126, 134
Khobar Towers bombing, 55–61, 126, 134
Kidnapping, 85–91

L

L-1 visas, 158
Labor Certification, 165–166
Labor Condition Application (LCA), 154–155
LaMonte-Shaban, Louis, 30–31
LaMonte-Shaban, Mariann, 30–31
Latino immigrants, 98
LCA (Labor Condition Application), 154–155
Lennon, John, 1–6, 33, 123
LGBTQ community, 118–119
Libya, 11–12, 107
Litvinenko, Alexander, 102
Local government, 114
Local law enforcement, 112, 114
    and international child abductions, 88
    and terrorism, 127–128
Lone Survivor (Luttrell), 72–74
Louisiana v. Neri Lopez, 113–114
Lozano v. Hazleton, 112–113
Luttrell, Marcus, 72–76

M

M-1 visas, 158

Marijuana, 2–4, 108
Marriage, 118–119
Materials witness visas, 162
Media
    dark side of, 35–40
    management of, 29–40, 95
    public opinion influenced by, 66, 75
    social media, 19
    strategic use of, 26–27, 49
    talk shows and, 34
    threats due to coverage, 58
    visas for representatives of, 156
Megrahi, Abdelbaset al-, 11
MI6, 56
Mossad (Mishal), 39
Muehler v. Mena, 114–115
Multinational executive visas, 164
Multinational manager visas, 164
Muslims
    deportation and, 130
    distrust of, in US, 23
    travel ban, 107

N

N visas, 159
Narcotics, 1, 3
National Automated Immigration Lookout Systems (NAILS), 38
National Interest Waiver, 165
National Security Agency (NSA), 100
Neumann, Janosh, 103–106
Neumann, Victoria, 103–106
9/11, 11, 23, 31, 54
    anti-Muslim sentiment and, 82
    and Pakistan, 79
    and Saudi Arabia, 51
    and undocumented immigrants, 62–66
    victims of, 62–66